D1156378

PRAISE FOR HAPPY ADVISOR

"In having the continuing opportunity to speak to thousands of financial advisors every year, I find that they respond to positive ideas from someone they trust. William Smith's book will stimulate your creative thinking, cause you to feel better about the challenges you confront and help you perform more effectively, while improving your results."
—Art Mortell, author and motivational speaker.

"The Happy Advisor is a tool that all financial professionals must have in their arsenal. Bill Smith is a master storyteller and jumps inside the heads of those who are on the firing line every day. He offers solutions and guidance with his hard-hitting stories, and is uniquely qualified to do so because he began in the trenches about 30 years ago. When Bill says 'I know you' in the first chapter—he means it from his heart. As a successful wealth manager, Bill's observations and advice to advisors and brokers are powerful and cut right to the underlying issues that they face in business every day. The Happy Advisor is a memorable and hands-on 'read' for new advisors right on up to C-level executives. Advisors will find themselves referring to Bill's book for years to come."
—Sydney LeBlanc, co-founder, *Registered Rep* magazine.

"Bill Smith's book is full of useful and practical ways to develop the crucial and important skills required to be a successful Financial Advisor. He shows us step by step how to literally achieve success in the financial services industry. Indeed it is the mother lode of our industry's principles. I recommend you read this book. You will be better off for having done so."
—Gene Ingargiola, former Senior Vice President Market Manager, Wachovia Securities

"I've been a Bill Smith fan for many years and I am thrilled he decided to write this book. His inspirational message and practical insights are sure to lift advisor spirits and client satisfaction. What makes Bill unique is his authenticity and ability to relate to the everyday challenges advisors face. Now more than ever, we need thought leaders like Bill Smith. Bravo! I am glad I know you."
—Bob David, President of Bob David Live Inc.

"I highly recommend The Happy Advisor *if you want to be both happy AND successful. Author Bill Smith, a 30+ year veteran advisor, is in the trenches just like you, so he KNOWS what challenges you face. This is an 'A to Z' primer on attitudinal fitness for your Financial Advisor career that gives you the tactics he uses every day to stay positive, confident and focused, especially in a difficult market. It's a 'must own' for your success library."*
—Jim "Da Coach" Rohrbach

"The Happy Advisor *is a must read for every advisor who is looking for solid success principals written by one of their own. Bill Smith has the unique ability to breakdown each idea and make it actionable today. Do yourself a huge service and add this book to your positive mental diet list."*
—Joe Lukacs, business coach and Bill Smith's coach

"Any FA can use Bill Smith's proven approaches to reinvigorate their business. This unique book is a one-of-a-kind resource you'll reach for again and again. The sage advice and advisor-centric examples will get you out of any rut and give you an unstoppable mindset for success."
—Edward Klink, business writer

THE HAPPY ADVISOR

BILL SMITH

Horsesmouth LLC

Horsesmouth, LLC.
21 West 38th Street
New York, NY 10018

For information contact:

Horsesmouth
21 West 38th Street
New York, NY 10018
1-888-336-6884. Outside the US: +1 (212) 343-8760
web: www.horsesmouth.com
e-mail: sales@horsesmouth.com

Horsesmouth books are available at special quantity discounts to use as promotions, or for use in corporate training programs. For more information, please contact Horsesmouth.

Horsesmouth can bring authors to your live event. For more information or to book an event, contact Horsesmouth at 1-888-336-6884. Outside the US: +1 (212) 343-8760.

FIRST EDITION

Designed by Russell Jones

ISBN-978-0-976804-7-2

Table of Contents

Men would likely still be living in caves if not for the women who nurture us, love us, and who make life worth living. I am fortunate to have three such women in my life: My mother June, my daughter Amber, and of course my wife Wanda. To the three most saintly, generous and remarkable women I know.

Acknowledgements

Dennis Drescher first believed in the idea that financial advisors would like to hear about more than just markets and products. Over the years, William Chettle and Johanna Fallon welcomed and edited many columns at my firm. Their encouragement was invaluable. Industry sage Sydney LeBlanc suggested that I submit articles to Horsesmouth. From that grew many columns and this book, to which I am indebted to genius editors Wendi Webb and Ed Klink, and Editor-in-Chief Sean Bailey, who was an enthusiastic fan of this project from the beginning, and expertly guided it to completion.

None of this would have been possible without the help of my own team: Christine Wilson has served me and my clients for about 20 years of my career. Michael Andreotti, my business partner, watched the store while I was out, and Joshua Jones reminded me that I'm not too old to learn new technology.

And lastly, I'd like to thank all of those who read the columns over the years and said that they were helped. Paul, Jason, Mark, Brad, Tony, and so many others...I'll never be able to express how much your kind words meant to me.

FOREWORD

During the dark days of 2008, as the financial markets collapsed and the Great Recession gained horrible downward momentum, the editors at Horsesmouth heard continually from advisors. The seemingly endless barrage of negative news and jaw-dropping changes to the market, the industry, and the world left nearly everyone unnerved and confounded. Advisors faced a test of their mettle unlike anything they'd ever experienced.

When clients panicked about the safety of their money market accounts and *The Wall Street Journal* declared on its front page "the end of Wall Street as we know it," you knew we'd reached a new level of awful.

Advisors needed help and guidance more than ever.

At Horsesmouth, we threw open our electronic doors and invited everyone in the industry to accept a special Bear Market Emergency Membership. We wanted everyone to benefit from the critical advice offered daily by expert contributors and writers as the crisis unfolded.

We especially faced the challenge of helping advisors maintain calmness and keep a good attitude while reaching out to clients and making tough calls. We needed to offer just the right words. And I knew this was a job for Bill Smith—full-time advisor and part-time Horsesmouth contributor.

For nearly a decade, Bill's Uncommon WYSdom column had delivered the kind of insights, authenticity, and energy that gave occasionally beleaguered advisors the courage to act.

And that's what we needed to deliver to advisors right away.

But Bill was an advisor first and foremost, with nearly 30 years of service. He had clients who needed help like everyone else. He was locked in the throes of responding to the crisis as best as he could. How could we expect him to turn out a column in these conditions and under this kind of pressure?

For several days, while the markets kept dropping, I could be heard in the Horsesmouth offices loudly asking over the din of CNBC, "What do we hear from Bill Smith? What do we hear from Bill Smith? We need a classic Bill Smith."

Of course, it was unrealistic to expect that he'd write a column in the middle of the biggest financial crisis of a generation.

But we kept asking with e-mails and voice mails. After a couple days of silence, we got a message: "I'll have something shortly."

Finally, on Oct. 8, 2008, Bill shipped a column and we rushed it out the very next day. It was titled "You Are Called to Duty for Such a Time as This." Within minutes of it appearing on Horsesmouth, the comments from advisors started pouring in:

- From St. Charles, Ill.: "This is what I needed to be

reminded of at this point in time. I have been in this business since 1984 but have never experienced the fear I have had this week, or month. But we do have words of wisdom for our clients; we just have to have the courage to call them."

- From Richmond, Va.: "Another great piece from Bill Smith! Thanks for YOUR call to duty by writing this article!"

- From Silverdale, Wash.: "Outstanding! This is what we need to be reminded of right now."

- From Greensboro, Ga.: "Thank you! Great article just when I needed some perspective!"

- From Oak Brook, Ill.: "Probably the best article that I have read from Horsesmouth and that is saying a lot since most of the articles are excellent."

- From Chesterfield, Mo.: "Wow, thank you Mr. Smith for reminding me what is most important today."

In the select world of writers called upon by editors to step up and deliver their best at exactly the right moment, Bill Smith had excelled.

But while I was overjoyed with his column and its response, I was not surprised. Time and again, for more than a decade now, Bill's columns have touched advisors deeply and motivated them to action.

Each time one graces our pages, we hear from our members—advisors like Bill Smith—who tell us Bill has put his finger on exactly the right words and right recommendations they needed to rethink a problem or re-energize their mindset.

Now we have collected these gems and edited them here for your inspiration and guidance under the title *The Happy Advisor*.

I recommend you keep this book nearby your desk and dip into it carefully, taking time to reflect on each of its passages over the weeks and months and years ahead.

You see, it is motivational dynamite. Handle it with care.

Sean M. Bailey

Editor-in-Chief
Horsesmouth
New York City
Aug. 8, 2010

1

An Advisor's Creed

When my son Eric was about 4 years old, he tried to pet an unfamiliar dog in the park. The dog barked at him, and Eric recoiled, surprised. After he composed himself, he looked up to me and concluded, "That doggie doesn't know my name."

In Eric's world, everyone who knew him and loved him called him by name. "Know my name" meant to him that someone understood him, loved him, and was friendly toward him.

I know your name. Or rather, I know you. Because you and I walk the same path daily.

I know that you're one of the tiny minority who is willing to take a job with no guarantees, no salary, and prosper by your wits, skills, and perseverance. That by itself puts you in the top 10%.

I know that you have watched people with more personality or better test scores fall by the wayside, make excuses, and leave the business, while you toughed it out. You are the one out of five who started on the same path and survived. That puts you in the top 2%.

I know you.

I know that you seldom read an industry publication or material from your firm that speaks your language (except maybe Horsesmouth). I know that you smile when you hear people who failed at what you do telling you how to do it.

I know that while the management of your firm sometimes sees you just as a thimble of water in a vast ocean, your clients see you as a trusted one-of-a-kind advisor. Someone who protects and serves, who cares more about them and their financial health than anyone else not related to them by blood.

I know you.

I know that although others may see you as a generic "producer on a plateau," you see yourself as someone who is lacing up his shoes to score more touchdowns than ever in this game. I know that in your heart, you still have it in you to become the top producer in your city, your region, or your firm, if you can just find the right combination of seminars, referral system, and daily activities. You've never given up. Not only that, but if the game were scored by how well you take care of your clients, you would already be in the hall of fame.

I know that you're a superhero. Superman can fly, but he

won't be there to give your clients great investment advice. Wonder Woman has a magic rope, but she's not going to be calling your clients to warn them about tax changes. Spider-Man has "spidey sense," but even after that radioactive spider bite, he doesn't have the super-hearing ability to detect exaggeration, illogic, and even falsehood about investments that you use to protect your clients. You have all those superpowers and many more. You are a real-life superhero with powers that matter.

I know you.

I know that you show up every day, through good times and bad, with happy clients and sad, ignore every fad, and produce business like mad.

I know that you've never seen a movie that portrays what you really do. Instead, Hollywood produces movies like "Wall Street," which promote an ugly caricature of what you do and who you are.

I know that you treat your clients as unique individuals. You know their nicknames, their cat's name, and their tennis partner's name. Yet sometimes you receive letters from people seeking your business who address you as Advisor #123.

I know you.

I know that although regulatory agencies think of you as a salesperson and at least one firm refers to you as its "distribution system," you often spend more of your time talking people out of investments than talking them into them. Daily, you act against your own financial interest to take care of the people entrusted to you. You spend time with young people or people with little money, making a gift of your knowledge.

I know that you've recommended an investment to a client that turned out wonderfully and smiled years later when that same client talked about his "great idea."

I know that your clients have become your friends. You've rejoiced with them when their children got into college, encouraged them when they were sick, and grieved with them at the loss of a family member.

I know you.

I know that you've seen the clowns on financial television and in the printed media talk nonsense, knowing that their main responsibility was to be entertaining in order to sell advertising—not to give sound advice. You've wished they would have to sit across a desk from people who took their bad recommendations and be accountable for it, as you are.

I know that you cope with the anxiety of a new month, financial worries, balance in your life, and challenges with your kids.

I know that you go to work every day in a job that requires excellent performance, even when you don't feel like it. You have to be upbeat like a stage performer, listen like a counselor, project the confidence of a drill instructor, and offer the professional selflessness of a doctor who gives her best advice regardless of how it is received.

I know you.

I know that you will run through walls for a manager who believes in you or a client who needs you.

I know that although you may seem of little importance to many people in the world, to someone, you are their whole world.

I know you and I respect you because you exhibit integrity, perseverance, and character quietly, every day, and outside the spotlight, where no one but you and those whom you serve see it.

I know that you do great things simply because it is who you are and you wouldn't consider living any other way.

I know you, and I'm proud to know you.

2

You Are Called to Duty for Such a Time as This

During an epidemic, an emergency-room doctor works 48 hours straight, risking her own health in order to treat a stream of sick, suffering patients that never seems to end.

In the fires raging through California, a firefighter works tirelessly, putting his own life on the line to fight fires attacking other people's homes and getting people to leave their homes against their loud protests. He doesn't mention that he's just heard that his own home has been ravaged by the fires.

An army sergeant serves a 14-month tour in Iraq, much of it in 120-degree heat. He is missing his wife and young family as he meets with Iraqi villagers to mediate their needs for water, power, and protection.

Why do these professionals do this? Because it is who they are. They are at the point of the spear. At times of crisis, they have the training, knowledge, and experience to take immediate, vital action. At other, less stressful times, these trained experts haven't had to make the same sacrifices—but when they are called to be superhuman, they answer that call.

Have you felt like that lately? You're talking to clients all day long, helping them through difficult times. You may be worried about your own mortgage, your children's college funds, or your retirement account. The company name on your front door may have changed several times last week. Your company stock may be worth a lot less than it was two weeks ago. And no one can tell you exactly what is next. Yet you stay focused on your clients.

FOR SUCH A TIME AS THIS

In one of the Bible's greatest tales of courage, a beautiful young Jewish girl, Esther, has just been named Queen of Persia when she learns of a plot afoot to kill all the Jews in the land. Esther is terrified for her family and herself. She hesitates to approach her new husband (who is unaware of her ancestry). The law forbids her from going to the king uninvited; doing so would be to risk her own life. Yet she does approach him to plead her case after talking to her guardian Mordecai, who issues her this sage challenge: "Who knows but that you have come to royal position for such a time as this?"

How many times in your life have you been placed somewhere important "for such a time as this?" We don't have to equate what we do with preventing genocide thousands of years ago, or with the life-and-death situations faced by doctors, firefighters, and our military to know that we are in a unique position to help now. The principle is the same.

RECALL YOUR VALUE

Your clients need you—not the pundits on television nor the geniuses at cocktail parties. You are in a position of trust, you can provide knowledge and a firm hand. You can't treat all the feverish investment patients in the world, but you can treat those who count on you. You can't put out every fire, but you can put out the ones burning in front of you right now. You know whether to take advantage of the opportunities this environment offers—or to advise your clients to hold steady.

Those of us who have been around at least three decades or so have seen five or six critical periods. After all, the biggest one-day market drop many of us have ever seen was 22% in one day in October 1987. It was also the biggest buying opportunity of our careers.

Since that time, someone who invested in the Dow would have seen their portfolio grow six-fold, even at periodic lower levels. Clients at that time all felt and expressed the same fears they invariably do at market bottoms: "This time is different." "Can the financial markets survive?" "It's never dropped like this before!" "But the bond and stock markets have both crashed!"

You're there, in position to do much good. No one else can do what you do with your clients. You may have 500 clients, but each of them has only one advisor. Make those calls, even to the "critically ill," to those whose "houses are on fire," and to those who need "wartime protection." And as you do so, remember a few actions to take at stressful times:

1. **Maintain self-care.** Take care of your own health. Exercise and get sufficient sleep.

2. **Know when to quit.** Work several extra hours if necessary, but don't work past exhaustion.

3. **Be kind.** Be kind to family, clients, and coworkers. No matter how angry or calm their voice, inside there is a frightened child asking, "Am I going to be OK?"

4. **Be kind to yourself** (emotionally).

BLAME GAME OVER

Don't harass yourself. For goodness' sake, stop blaming yourself. Maybe you could have done something different for your clients, but it is a debilitating time waster to worry about that right now. At times of crisis, the doctor doesn't beat herself up over why she didn't give more flu shots, nor the fireman lament that he didn't tell more people to cut the brush around their home. Here are some additional ways to remain proactive in tense situations:

- **Stay grateful.** Take out a journal or a notebook and write down five things for which you're grateful every day.

- **Get motivated.** Pull out or buy a motivational book or CD. Read or listen before you go to work every day.

- **Talk about it.** Don't be a silo, with everything kept inside. You can lean on others, and just talking it out will help relieve some pressure.

- **Recognize support.** Cherish and never forget those clients and friends who ask you at this time, "How are you doing?"

- **Call your people.** It matters to them, and they will remember whether you do or don't.

- **Be growth-seeking.** Take one courageous action every day. It doesn't have to be anything huge—maybe it's just picking up the phone.

- **Capitalize on opportunities.** Many an advisor has rescued people who are not hearing from the people who should be calling them right now.

- **Pay extra close attention to details.** This is not the time to have an order error or fail to return a client's phone call. Keeping track of the small stuff maintains and deepens clients' trust.

- **Remember, this too shall pass.** But it will only work to your benefit and your clients' benefit if you are fully engaged right now. If you stay on task, in a few years you may see client accounts and your production both at a multiple of where they are now.

For such a time as this...

3

Rethink Your Attitude in the New Year

Experts and industry veterans can talk endlessly about the benefits of business planning—but myriad advisors remain unconvinced. After all, concrete planning is much trickier and more time-consuming than wishful thinking. Then again, wishful thinking doesn't work.

There's a difference, of course, between a pipe dream and a positive attitude; top producers cite optimism as critical to their success. How can you diagnose a case of wishful—versus positive—thinking? Let's outline some of the chief symptoms of wishful-thinking syndrome:

- Wishing the market would act like it used to, rather than adapting your strategies to the current situation.

- Waiting until you're motivated to create a great day, rather than reading a book or listening to a motivating recording in order to put yourself in a great frame of mind.

- Hoping that wealthy, pleasant prospects with money call you based on your tremendous reputation in the community, rather than setting appointments with centers of influence to remind them of what you do.

- Expecting clients to call with their ideas, rather than calling them to ask questions about their needs.

- Waiting for CNBC to become positive and motivate investors throughout the community to invest, rather than calling clients and proactively making the case for buying now.

- Believing that adversity is bad and cannot be overcome, rather than seeing a roadblock as an amazing opportunity. Thomas Carlyle, Scottish social commentator, remarked, "The block of granite, which was an obstacle in the path of the weak, becomes a stepping stone in the path of the strong."

- Being certain that a low market is an awful thing—not an opportunity—as veteran advisors have tried to tell you about 2009, 2002, 1987, 1982, and 1974.

- Wishing for a more understanding branch manager, less paperwork, more television ads, and free leads, rather than working your way through it all like that successful advisor down the hall who doesn't really seem to know that he shouldn't be doing well.

- Waiting for the winds of business to become more favorable, rather than turning the rudder of your own ship and tacking into the wind.

UNWISHING THE WISHFUL THINKING

Now here are a few examples of a productive, positive approach:

- Playing with the team you have, not the team you wish you had.

- Playing with the cards you were dealt, not the cards you wish you had been dealt.

- Recognizing that "Every adversity, every failure, every heartache contains within it the seed of an equivalent or a greater benefit."
  —Napoleon Hill

- Realizing that "Failing with an excuse—even a really, really good excuse—is never as good as succeeding."
  —Bill Bachrach

4

Become a Top Producer in 21 Days

At a critical point in my summer sales job while in college, I received a little yellow booklet in the mail from my sales manager. It was entitled "The Common Denominator of Success." It only ran about 12 pages, but I'll never forget what it said.

This pocket-sized pamphlet was the transcript of a speech given by Albert E. N. Gray, an insurance company executive, in 1940. You can still find the full text on the Internet. Gray had spent years interviewing and studying successful people, trying to learn the secrets of their success. The people he interviewed seemed to achieve success whether they were highly intelligent or just ordinary. While some people worked hard all their lives and retired poor, others, with apparently less effort, were able to reach extraordinary heights. What was the common denominator for those who succeeded? His conclusion was:

"Successful people form the habit of doing the things that unsuccessful people don't like to do."

I can still remember his logic: What are the things that unsuccessful people don't like to do? The same things that everyone else doesn't like to do! Things like cold calling, handling details, asking for the order, showing courage, or operating outside our comfort zones.

HABIT FORMING SUCCESS

OK, so successful people do the things we don't like to do. Big deal. How does that help you and me do all the things we need to do to succeed? The answer lies in three little words: "form the habit." Successful people do the things that others avoid, and they do them as a matter of habit. The beauty of even a difficult habit is that, once it is formed, it is easier to keep it up than to break. Successful people form the proper habits, and they no longer have to make a decision every day about whether to tackle those difficult items. They just do it by habit.

How does that apply to us? Well, experts say it takes 21 consecutive days to form a habit. Three weeks of 25 contacts a day, and you will find it hard not to make those contacts. Twenty-one days of asking for three referrals a day, and you'll feel something missing if you don't ask for the third one on the 22nd day. Form the habit of coming in early, and you will move heaven and earth to get there. Form the habit of writing your call list the day before, and you will break into a cold sweat if it isn't done.

Sow an act, and you reap a habit. Sow a habit, and you reap a character. Sow a character, and you reap a destiny.
—Charles Reade

5

Ten Ways to Break Out of a Slump

A baseball slugger goes 3 days without a hit. Your NFL team's quarterback gets sacked three times in a row. Meryl Streep doesn't feel like appearing in front of the camera. We've all had slumps. But as the saying goes, "only the mediocre are always at their best."

What are some proven ways to break out of a slump?

1. **Always keep records.** Psychologists say that "self-actualizing" people like us cannot keep records of an activity—such as exercise, contacts, or referrals—without bettering their performance. They will either improve or stop keeping records. The cognitive dissonance becomes too much.

2. **Realize that slumps are natural.** The tide comes in; the tide goes out. Don't annualize your slump or your good times. Projecting the most recent trend into the future is what economists do—it's way too passive for a dynamic person like you.

3. **Work on action, and ignore results for a while.** The law of averages will pay off. Baseball sluggers like Babe Ruth and Ted Williams kept swinging because, although they knew that action might not produce results, they also knew that inaction would certainly not achieve anything.

4. **Think of three reasons a slump is good for you.** Suffering a slump builds character; it means that time off doesn't cost you much; it helps you focus on other priorities, and so forth. W. Clement Stone said that the Depression was the best thing that ever happened to him because it taught him discipline. He went on to run a $2 billion company and give over $275 million to charity.

5. **Give back.** A slump may actually be the boost you need, says Coach Shawn Greene, of Savage & Greene in a Horsesmouth discussion forum. Volunteer to help someone you wouldn't usually help—not one of your usual prospects. Or speak to a group that needs your guidance. This

very experience may remind you of your own expertise and the good you do.

6. **Get some perspective, hermanos y hermanas!** (That means brothers and sisters.) I recently went on a trip to a very poor, communist country where the average wage is $9 per month. That's for laborers, doctors, everyone. And the people deal with it, love their families, help their friends, and are reasonably happy. No matter what kind of slump you think you're in, I can give you a list of people who would trade places with you.

7. **Think bigger!** Don't just get back to your previous level of performance; blow right through it. Bill Nicklin, giant producer, former branch manager, and Horsesmouth co-founder, says he saw an advisor in a slump begin really prospecting people in a particular niche and move from $300,000 in annual production to over $2 million a few years later.

8. **Fight FEAR.** Harry A. Olson, in the Horsesmouth slump discussion forum, says fear is "False Evidence Appearing Real." It's overgeneralization with a failure to discriminate. The experience of fear makes you feel weak and believe that your well is dry. The fear response is biologically wired in the brain. It impairs working memory.

9. **Win the battle.** How proud would you feel if you could beat a three-year-old at arm wrestling? Not very. How about if you beat Arnold Schwarzenegger? The bigger the battle, the bigger the prize. As my youngest son says, "Pain is temporary. Glory is forever. Chicks dig scars."

10. **Remember what you've learned.** And next time, when you hit a slump, maybe you'll be languishing at a level that would have been your record production a few years earlier.

6

From Good Advisor to Great Advisor: What Makes the Difference?

As the old adage goes, "Good is the enemy of great." How's your business? Good? How would you like to make it great?

In Jim Collins' runaway bestseller, *Good to Great*, the former Stanford faculty member describes the unique characteristics of companies whose earnings and stock value went from plateau to mountain chart over sustained periods of time. Or since advisors are numbers people, let's say it this way: The 11 companies that made his cut "attained extraordinary results, averaging cumulative stock returns 6.9 times the general market in the fifteen years following their transition points." CEOs and managers have marveled at his findings for years now.

Collins' basic finding was that in each of the 11 companies that met his parameters, the CEOs were humble, unbelievably committed, and disciplined. They brought in the right people to build a disciplined procession toward their core value. Out of the 11 companies that made it through his filter, not a one had a CEO who was a household name. Not a Jack Welch or Lee Iacocca in the bunch. No management rock stars—but a lot of real virtuosos when it comes to getting results.

WHAT DO THE GREAT FOLK DO?

What does it take for advisors to move their practices from good to great like these companies? What do those who transition to greatness do that those who remain merely good don't? After 30 years of being an advisor and decades of studying high-achieving advisors who have turned the corner from good to great, here are my conclusions on what you need to do:

FIND YOUR BURNING DESIRE AND RENEW IT DAILY

The people at the model companies in *Good to Great* have a passion for what they do. To be constantly motivated is not a natural state in our world. I'm told that by the time we are 16, we have had 10 times as much negative input as positive input. And that's our baseline! Add to that getting cut off in traffic, discount broker ads ridiculing your very existence, and complex or challenging markets, and it's no wonder advisors are just not naturally motivated. The great companies and the great financial advisors write down their clear goals, read them every morning, and listen to a motivational or inspirational CD on the way to work every day. The great Zig Ziglar, in reply to someone who suggested that motivation doesn't last, said, "Neither does bathing, but it's still a good idea to do it every day!"

STRIVE FOR CONSISTENTLY EXCELLENT DAYS

"Excellent days add up to excellent weeks, which add up to excellent months, which add up to excellent years. A series of excellent years creates an excellent career," says Joe Lukacs, business coach and Horsesmouth contributor. As advisors, we have a calling with unlimited potential, but where the only real discipline or accountability is self-imposed. If you and I don't plan and control our actions, one after another, then someone else will: a client calling, other people stopping by, the market, and so forth.

Top producers answer the question, "What one thing, if it were done consistently and excellently, would change my business and my life?" It could be a high number of telephone dials, asking for referrals, or getting exercise. Then they act on it, and do that "one thing" first, until it is a habit. Once that is a habit, they ask the question again. Everyone knows the truth of the 80/20 principle, that 20% of their activities produce 80% of the results, but how many of us systematically double the amount of time spent in those 20% activities? Top producers think this way. They look again to see what the top 20% activities are and repeat the process. They may even set up accountability to another person such as a friend or a coach in order to get started.

Now here's Jim Collins' illustration as it relates to excellent days: "Picture a huge, heavy flywheel—a metal disk mounted horizontally on an axle, about 30 feet in diameter, 2 feet thick, and weighing about 5,000 pounds. Now imagine that your task is to get the flywheel rotating on the axle as fast and long as possible." As he describes it, with great effort you begin pushing the flywheel. It may take you an hour to get it to go around once. In fact, its motion may be almost imperceptible. But then the next hour, building on its own momentum, you are able to spin it around twice. Within a few days or weeks, with constant pushing, it is spinning at thousands of revolutions an hour, maybe thousands a minute. And that's all because each motion builds on the past momentum. It's the same with habits of the excellent day.

KNOW YOUR NICHE

Collins retells an Isaiah Berlin story about the fox and the hedgehog. "The fox knows many things, but the hedgehog knows one big thing." When the fox jumps out of the bushes, the hedgehog just rolls into a ball, protected on all sides by his spikes. The fox may nose around a bit, but in the end, he goes away. Management at the top companies profiled in *Good to Great* know exactly what business they are about and they remain focused on it, come what may. Good companies and advisors may move from fad to fad or product to product. The great ones find a niche—be it a product, a service, or a type of market to serve—and they dominate it.

COMMAND YOUR TIME

In *Good to Great,* Collins notes that executives at his 11 winning companies deliberately choose specific technology to meet their goals, but they are not in love with technology.

They just look at it as a tool. For advisors, the one essential tool is an effective contact management system. And you have to be an expert with it; you have to know who you've talked to, when, and the next time to contact them. You need notes on what's important to them, what your last conversations were about, and you need the ability to write to them often. Prospects and clients are your lifeline. Any advisor who doesn't have a good contact system but who will commit to learning one and using it can get an immediate 20% increase in production. And here's the serendipitous benefit: Some of us advisors aren't prospecting or opening new accounts because our memories just aren't what they used to be. We can't pack in one more John and Mary Jones and their jobs and their kids' names and what's important to them. Well, the contact management system can record all that stuff, so you never have to worry about remembering it again. (Or be embarrassed because you forgot it.)

MOVE TO MANAGED MONEY

Moving clients' assets to a fee-based platform has tremendous advantages. I'm just not sure they're the same ones that proponents suggest. Let me share two sometimes neglected reasons why managed money can be so significant in moving from good to great:

"You can only take so many body blows." I heard this from a branch office manager who runs an office in New York City with 40 million-dollar producers. That's the office minimum, and there is a waiting list! Brett Favre, living-legend quarterback, has been sacked hundreds of times. And that's just in his pro career, not college or high school. How many more can he take? He's pretty tough, but who really knows? The better question is, How many more can you take? How many times in a day or in your career can you be rejected and jump back up for the next play? Managed money requires work but allows you to take your body blows in prospecting or asking for referrals, rather than in calling clients for transactions every day.

It combines the best of timeless investment principles with modern portfolio science. (In fact, that would be a pretty good elevator speech, wouldn't it?) Try as we might, it's hard to get individual client portfolios up to the efficient-frontier line on our own. Clients don't want to sell winners, and they do want to sell temporary losers (or vice versa when it comes to buying). Often, they only want to do what the media tell them is popular. Managed money can help solve that problem.

BUILD A SOLID TEAM

Some companies move from good to great when they create a strong team. Collins says that all of the companies that moved from good to great first began with getting the right people on the bus. In most cases, they did this even before they had decided what their market focus was going to be. They knew that they were going to have to be responsive to change, and that if they had the best people, they could adapt and adjust and have a great company. Plus it was a lot more fun to be surrounded by eagles than turkeys. In our business, having a team, even if it's only two people, allows advisors to use the 80/20 principle, spending our time on the most important (not most urgent) activities. I go back and forth on whether my client account administrator, Christine Wilson, is awesome or stupendous. I think she's both. I'm fascinated that she loves to do things that are not my strengths, such as organizing files. We have a rule that I am never allowed to have an original of a document, because it may disappear in a pile of papers, never to be seen again. Are you using your strengths and getting help on your weaknesses?

Want to move from Good to Great? Learn from those who have done it!

7

Twelve Points to Soothe Your Rattled Psyche

Elsewhere in this book, we list 10 talking points for jittery clients in volatile times. But dispelling clients' anxiety can be easy compared with your other challenge: keeping your own nerves in check.

If you're earning less than you used to—and spending your days talking to frustrated investors, feeling sorry for them, trying to give answers that even you only half believe, losing hope, and not seeing any light at the end of the tunnel—what might you possibly say to yourself to boost your spirits? Here are some suggestions:

1. **Look forward.** "I can't wait to see how excited my clients will be when we finally have a 10% 'up' year!"

2. **Look back.** "If I could revisit 1982, I would tell an advisor to buy with both hands when the DJIA dropped to 750, because 20, 30 or 40 years later, even at the bottom of another bear market, the index would still be up 1000%."

3. **Look for the silver (on)lining.** "During the dot-com boom, I would have given anything if someone had said that I would never again hear the 'online trading' objection, right? So what am I complaining about?"

4. **Focus on opportunity #1.** "Once there was a genie who told a man that if he would walk along the beach that night and fill his pockets with pebbles, he would be both happy and sad in the morning. And in the morning, he found the genie was right. All the pebbles he had collected the night before were, in reality, rubies, emeralds, and other precious stones. He was happy to have the stones, but sad that he did not pick up more. How many new clients could I be putting in my pockets now? Imagine how their portfolios could look in a few years."

5. **Focus on opportunity #2.** "So let me get this right: 10%, 20%, 30% of my competition is leaving the business. Why is this not a good thing?"

6. **Focus on opportunity #3.** "Most people I prospect are unhappy with their investments and their advisor. No amount of advertising could have created this salutary circumstance."

7. **You're more than the Dow Jones.** "My clients need me for advice unrelated to the market. Someone will need me to help them plan their estate. Someone else will need me to explain IRA rollover rules. No telling what kind of advice they might get were I not here to help them."

8. **Success is forged from fire.** "One extremely successful advisor was asked years ago if he had enjoyed a smooth, gradual rise in production over the years. 'No way. A lot of difficult times. I even refinanced my home twice.' In the words of the old 'Facts of Life' theme song, 'You take the good, you take the bad....'"

9. **Remember that the market and our own emotions are just a succession of cycles.** "I tell myself that 'This too shall pass.'"

10. **Kwitcher bellyachin.** "For goodness sake, how tough is my job really? Blind people and a paraplegic man have climbed El Capitan, the 3,300-foot vertical granite wall at Yosemite. Now that's a challenge."

11. **Learn from it.** "A man going through tough times once asked his minister when his present difficulties would be over. The minister replied, 'When you've finished learning all that you're supposed to learn from it.' Have I learned all that I'm supposed to learn from this bear market?"

12. **You're golden.** "Gold is refined and purified by fire. Wood and straw are destroyed. I am gold."

How to Get the Respect You Deserve

Respect. Martial arts expert Chuck Norris, singer Aretha Franklin, and comedian Rodney Dangerfield built their careers around it. Norris commands it, Franklin demands it, and Dangerfield famously never got it.

"Let me tell you, I don't get no respect," Dangerfield would lament, pulling his tie and glaring at you with bugged-out eyes. "When I was a kid, my dad carried around the picture of the kid who came with the wallet!"

Norris delivers over-the-top physical prowess. "There is no theory of evolution," they say, "just a list of animals that Chuck Norris allows to live." And when Aretha stalks the stage in stilettos belting out her hit song "Respect," you know she deserves it.

We all want to feel more like the masterful Norris or empowered Franklin than the victim Dangerfield. But how do we cultivate the feeling that we inherently deserve and will receive respect? That's an elusive goal, especially in a world where disrespect runs rampant:

- A veteran advisor changes branches. Now, rather than working with people who know and respect him, he's reduced to e-mail and telephone calls to people who couldn't pick him out of a police lineup. He is treated like a rookie and feels disrespected.

- Another advisor spends a day angry at a client because after spending an hour working on the client's request for documents, when he calls the client to tell him it is completed, the client says, "Forget it. I handled it another way." He feels angry and disrespected. He's just short of calling the client back and setting him straight.

Just how important is this human need for respect?

5 RESULTS OF DISRESPECT

1. An inner-city youth who gets "dissed" by someone on the street may resort to violence to regain his due respect.

2. A doctor flies into road rage because he doesn't feel respected when another car cuts him off.

3. When a football player makes a disrespectful comment about that week's opponent, the newspaper clipping that quotes him is pinned up in his adversary's locker room and results in some extra-hard hits.

4. Nations have gone to war over feeling disrespected.

5. Family members have refused to talk to each other for decades over perceived slights that they chose to remain angry and bitter about.

The search for respect can be never ending and unproductive, yet it is surprisingly common. In our business, advisors sometimes change firms because they feel they're not treated respectfully. Or they stay at the same firm and stew and stay bitter, lowering their own incomes and causing themselves health problems. Or their production hits a plateau when they don't make the phone calls they need to make because they are avoiding the potential disrespect of clients and prospects.

This search for the world's respect can pervade everything. It's one reason people go into debt to buy a $70,000 car when a $20,000 vehicle will get them there. It's a big piece of why people live in the neighborhoods they do, send their kids to the schools they do, and cover their walls with plaques. It's a component of why Boy Scouts strive for badges, soldiers earn ribbons, and students get advanced degrees ("I'll feel respected when they call me 'doctor.'"). It's why a 50-year-old accountant revs his Harley as he motors through a small town in the Midwest. Respect, man.

Yet can we really control other people's respect? One person reveres the Harley while another laughs. One neighbor considers that pricey car a prize; another finds it embarrassing and showy. Certainly at times, we will find ourselves around people who don't know us well enough to respect us. Many people will simply be indifferent to us. If we let ourselves depend on what others think, we are held hostage by their wide-ranging and ever-changing actions and opinions.

What's an advisor to do? There is a way to cultivate lasting respect, but it all starts on the inside.

PUTTING RESPECT IN PERSPECTIVE

1. **Show respect to others.** One father's advice to his daughter when dating was to evaluate a prospective boyfriend not by how he treated her, but by how he treated waiters. I'll bet you know assistants who are giving their advisors half-hearted support because the advisors continually treat them with disrespect. Whether you explain it through religious values, karma, or the golden rule, there is much to be gained by making it a personal policy to respect others.

2. **Remind yourself that it's not about you.** You will never be good enough or important enough that *everyone* will treat you with respect. Some people are busy with their own lives, some haven't developed people skills, and others simply may be selfish goons. Just be grateful that you're not one of them! My friend Dan runs short-term medical missions to the middle of the jungle. People who know him respect him greatly. One day, he parked in front of a convenience store, bought a soda, and then went next door to a pet store. The convenience store manager had his car towed from the customers-only space he was in. No respect. But Dan didn't let the store manager's opinion of him—and inconsiderate actions—color what he thinks of himself.

3. **Understand that it's the system, not the person.** Why does the tattooed Generation Y Starbucks employee greet you cheerfully and pay close attention to

your order, while a retail store employee ignores you completely to continue a conversation with a friend as you stand there, money in hand? They're both hired from the same labor pool, but the Starbucks system teaches people to give what they call "legendary service," while the retail store doesn't. Not only is it often not about you, sometimes it's not really about the other person, either. It's just about the system you're both operating in.

4. **Get stronger by building up your respect muscle.** Every time you decline to react negatively to a perceived slight, you become stronger and more mature. When you locate your sense of self-respect, you can handle more of the world's vagaries. Motivational speaker Art Mortell says that success in our business is directly related to the amount of rejection we can handle. We learn to handle more rejection by successfully handling more rejection—we build up our rejection-handling muscles so that they carry us through. We don't get mad, we don't take it personally, we don't feel disrespected, we just take it in stride and move on.

5. **Realize that it happens to everybody.** And I mean everybody. The first President Bush tells the story about the time that a man said to him, "Anybody ever tell you that you look like President Bush?" When the president admitted that sometimes they did, the man said, "Bet it makes you mad, don't it?" If disrespect can happen to a former president of the United States, it's going to happen to you and me.

6. **Drop out of the "respect game."** Since what different people will respect is so variable and depends so much on factors you can't control, why not just drop out of the competition for respect entirely? Instead, decide what it takes for you to respect yourself. To the degree that you do that successfully, you become immune to the actions of others. I once sat at a meeting next to a quiet, unassuming man and only discovered at dinner that night that he was the top producer in my firm of over 10,000 advisors. It wasn't so bad that I didn't notice, but none of the people running the meeting seemed to be aware of it either. But it didn't bother this fellow, because he was playing the respect game on his terms, not on anyone else's.

7. **Reframe your thinking.** Affirmations and better questions can change the way you experience yourself. What if you replace, "I've got to be a top producer to be worthy of respect," with "I feel good about what I am accomplishing, and the people I help are extremely important." How does it feel to ask, "How much is this client worth to me?" versus "Right now, with this client, what can I do to provide legendary service and make her feel important?"

8. **Go tell someone else how much you respect him.** Tell someone you respect that he reminds you of the classic Teddy Roosevelt speech "The Man in the Arena." Tell someone that after watching him, you think that where other people have backbones, he must have steel. Send someone you admire a note about the professional way she conducts her business; tell her

that if something ever happened to you, she's the kind of advisor you'd want your family to have. Give respect to those you admire and those who make the world a better place. Most people are lucky if they hear they're admired five times in a lifetime. Give that gift to someone once today.

FINAL THOUGHTS

In his book *Further Along the Road Less Traveled*, Dr. M. Scott Peck reminds us of Shelley's poem "Ozymandias," which describes a statue inscribed thus at the base:

"My name is Ozymandias, King of Kings:

Look on my works, ye Mighty, and despair!"

But only the pedestal and shattered remains of a colossal figure are found in the desert wasteland. No one remembers who the man was or what worldly wonders he accomplished.

It's not about the externals or what other people think. Respect is about what you think about yourself. Live your life not to impress others, but to earn your own respect. What a valuable and inexhaustible gift that is; doing what gives you self-respect is totally under your control. So even if the outside world doesn't quite get you, you can fully understand the wonderful, disciplined, honest, courageous, and accomplished person you are yourself. That no one can take away. And no one, except you, can give it to you, either.

9

Clients Think They Don't Need You? They're Wrong and Here's Why

These days we've moved beyond the discussion of why investors need our advice instead of doing it on their own. However, as we work through the loss of faith in analysts, institutions, and accountants, clients may be listening to advice from third parties and other unconventional sources. Have you ever thought about why investors need to hear you instead of listening to other professionals who may not be in the financial field?

5 REASONS CLIENTS NEED YOU

1. **There's no one like you.** They need you instead of other full-service advisors because you know you are honest and looking out for their interest. You can't be sure that other people will have the same kind of integrity or commitment.

2. **Third parties can be deadly to portfolios.** I have yet to hear a client mention that his neighbor suggested he buy stocks when the market is low. At the time of this writing, as usual, neighbors are telling people to buy bonds because they have been going up. A few years ago, they were bragging about their tech stocks, which were about to crater.

Never be bashful about telling your client that excellence or intelligence in one field does not translate to excellence in another field. If you need an example, just take a look at doctors' portfolios.

Counter erroneous advice immediately. When faced with an absurd suggestion from a third party, protect yourself with a couple of rebuttals. Years ago, a prospect who had sold his construction business smugly asked a young, quick-thinking advisor, "How much money do you have? Why should I listen to you about investing if I'm wealthier than you are?" The advisor replied: "I never thought of it that way. Now that I think of it, why don't we both turn our money over to Michael Jackson or Madonna, because they're wealthier than either of us?"

You can also attack the advice head-on. Let's say a neighbor, Ms. Jones, has pushed your client to get into a particular investment vehicle. Try this: "Did Ms. Jones mention which investment licenses she holds? Where she keeps her investment research department? We have responsibility for the appropriateness of our advice, and I will be sitting here next year, five, 10 years from now accountable to you and your family for this advice. How about Ms. Jones? Did she mention what responsibility she is willing to take for this advice?"

3. **You do more than count Morningstar stars.** You have the experience of advising hundreds of investors and accepting the consequences. You have the excellent judgment that has enabled you not to be voted off financial advisors' island. You have the courage to tell them not to buy a particular investment. And you have the backbone to stand up for your opinions, both in person and on the phone. Has a financial journalist returned their calls lately to talk about the poor performance of a mutual fund his magazine touted?

4. **You have the resources of a major investment firm backing you up.** If clients want to deal with people without your training, education, and experience in completely different areas, fine. There is no law to prevent them from hiring a plumber to draw up the architectural plans for their new home. But they should have no illusions about what they are doing and the possible ramifications.

5. **We are the major leagues.** If they want to deal with the minor leagues, fine. But we are where big, experienced, serious money goes to find a home and to sleep at night. Like an experienced river guide, you don't have to worry about the markets. You've seen them before and you know you will come out the other end. Now you can use your wisdom and experience to help your clients enjoy the ride.

10

Eighty Things You Do for Clients

Generally, I get two kinds of questions when people hear what I do: "What's the market going to do?" and "Know any hot stocks?"

My honest (and correct) answers never seem to satisfy them. To the first, I always answer: "Short term, I don't know what the market is going to do—and neither do all those people on television who loudly profess to know with certainty. Long term, I imagine it will do what it always has, which is to return 10%–12% per year, in fits and starts."

To the second question about hot stocks, I always answer: "Since I believe that the market is relatively efficient, and that all information about all stocks shows in the price of the stocks, I have no hot stocks to suggest. But a diversified portfolio of quality stocks has tended to outperform most other investment choices over time."

Well, finally, I got tired of these questions and decided to put together answers to the question: "What do you do?" Although this list is not exhaustive, I became exhausted just thinking about all the services we provide and stopped at 80. Maybe you'll agree with me and even add your own answers to this list.

WHAT A PROFESSIONAL ADVISOR DOES:

FINANCIAL PLANNING

1. Cares about you and your money as much as a good family doctor cares about you and your health.

2. Asks questions in order to understand your needs and objectives.

3. Helps you determine where you are at present.

4. Guides you to think about areas of your financial life you may not have considered.

5. Helps organize your financial situation.

6. Formalizes your goals and puts them in writing for you.

7. Helps you prioritize your financial opportunities.

8. Helps you determine realistic goals.

9. Studies possible alternatives that could meet your goals.

10. Prepares a financial plan and/or an investment policy statement for you.

11. Makes specific recommendations to help you meet your goals.

12. Implements those recommendations.

13. Suggests creative alternatives that you may not have considered.

14. Reviews and recommends life insurance policies to protect your family.

15. Assists you in setting up a company retirement plan.

16. Prepares a financial plan for you.

17. Assists in preparing an estate plan for you.

18. Reviews your children's custodial accounts and 529 plans.

19. Helps you determine your IRA Required Minimum Distribution.

20. Persuades you to do the things you know you ought to do, even if you don't feel like doing them.

INVESTMENTS

21. Prepares an asset allocation for you so you can achieve the best rate of return for a given level of risk tolerance.

22. Does due diligence on money managers and mutual fund managers in order to make appropriate recommendations.

23. Stays up-to-date on changes in the investment world.

24. Monitors your investments.

25. Reviews your existing annuities.

26. Reviews your investments in your company 401(k) or 403(b) plans.

27. Reviews your existing IRAs.

28. Reviews and revises portfolios as conditions change.

29. Guides you through difficult periods in the stock market by sharing historical perspective.

30. Improves your investment performance.

31. Looks "inside" your mutual funds to compare how many of their holdings duplicate each other.

32. Converts your investments to lifetime income.

33. Helps you evaluate the differences in risk levels between various fixed-income investments such as government bonds and corporate bonds.

34. Charts the maturities of your fixed-income investments.

35. Helps handle exchanges, tenders, and special stock dividends.

36. Holds and warehouses stocks, bonds, and other securities.

37. Records and researches your cost basis on securities.

38. Provides you with unbiased stock research.

39. Provides you with personal stock analysis.

40. Provides you with a written sector-based evaluation of your portfolio.

41. Determines the risk level of your existing portfolio.

42. Helps you consolidate and simplify your investments.

43. Can provide you with technical, fundamental, and quantitative stock analysis.

44. Gives you strategies for trading options.

45. Provides you with alternative investment options.

46. Provides you with executive services involving restricted stock and employer stock options.

47. Provides introductions to money managers.

48. Shows you how to access your statements and other information online.

49. Shops for top CD rates from financial institutions throughout the country.

50. Provides access to answers from a major investment firm.

TAXES

51. Suggests alternatives to lower your taxes during retirement.

52. Reviews your tax returns with an eye to possible savings in the future.

53. Stays up to date on tax law changes.

54. Helps you reduce your taxes.

55. Repositions investments to take full advantage of tax law provisions.

56. Works with your tax and legal advisors to help you meet your financial goals.

PERSON TO PERSON

57. Monitors changes in your life and family situation.

58. Proactively keeps in touch with you.

59. Remains only a telephone call away to answer financial questions for you.

60. Serves as a human glossary of financial terms such as beta, P/E ratio, and Sharpe ratio.

61. Makes sure that she and her firm provide excellent service at all times.

62. Provides referrals to other professionals, such as accountants and attorneys.

63. Refers you to banking establishments for loan and trust alternatives.

64. Provides you with a chart showing the monthly income from all of your investments.

65. Suggests alternatives to increase your income during retirement.

66. Listens and provides feedback in a way that a magazine or newsletter writer does not.

67. Shares the experience of dozens or hundreds of his clients who have faced circumstances similar to yours.

68. Helps educate your children and grandchildren about investments and financial concepts.

69. Holds seminars to discuss significant and/or new financial concepts.

70. Helps with the continuity of your family's financial plan through generations.

71. Facilitates the transfer of investments from individual names to trust, or from an owner through to beneficiaries.

72. Keeps you on track.

73. Identifies your savings shortfalls.

74. Develops and monitors a strategy for debt reduction.

75. Educates you on retirement issues.

76. Educates you on estate planning issues.

77. Educates you on college savings and financial aid options.

78. Is someone you can trust and get advice from in all your financial matters.

79. Is a wise sounding board for ideas you are considering.

80. Is honest with you.

11

'A' Is for Attitude

The greatest discovery of our time is that a man can change his life by changing the way he thinks.
—William James, psychologist and philosopher

A man is about as happy as he makes up his mind to be.
—Abraham Lincoln

One's attitude at the beginning of a task, more than any other single factor, determines the outcome.
—Napoleon Hill, *Think and Grow Rich*

Why is attitude important in our business? If we wait for outside events to improve our attitude, we'll have an awfully inconsistent record. Markets drop, traffic slows, weather turns bad, friends ignore us, clients leave, and our spouse doesn't understand us. Yet we need to approach each day with a positive expectancy. Or maybe not every day, just each day that ends in "y." If our attitude determines our success, then do we just wait for those days when we have a good attitude to go into work?

ATTITUDE ADJUSTMENT

Thankfully, there are things we can do to manage and create a good attitude. Here are 10 quick, simple 'tude-tuning techniques you can apply right now:

1. **Act positive and assumptive.** Although your actions can follow your feelings, your feelings can also follow your actions. Raise your head high, take a deep breath, smile, and see if you feel anything but positive. Your mind will pick up on the cues from your body.

2. **Walk the walk.** When you're going somewhere, watch how people move out of the way for someone who looks like she knows where she is going. Only 2% of people have a sense of urgency. Cultivate yours.

3. **Talk the talk.** When you ask someone, "How are you doing?" how often do you hear, "Pretty good for a Monday," or "Not bad, considering." I have an optometrist friend whose signature answer is, "Happy and enthusiastic!" No wonder he was a top athlete in high school and college, and became famous for his charitable work. Why not answer, "How are you doing?" with "Great! But it'll get better!" or "If I was doing any better, I'd have to be two people."

4. **Hang around positive people.** You wouldn't place your desk next to a sewer, would you? Why would you spend time with people who pollute your mind and their own?

5. **Speak well of other people.** The winners I know absolutely refuse to say anything bad about anyone. They speak highly of everyone they know.

6. **Read motivational books every day.** You wouldn't go a day without eating, so why go a day without feeding your mind? If you need some motivational references, consider *The Magic of Thinking Big*, by David J.

Schwartz, or *See You At the Top*, by Zig Ziglar.

7. **Listen to positive audio.** I mentioned this to a group of newly minted advisors in our New York office and pointed down to an audio CD store we could see from the office window. One advisor went out and bought some CD's that day, listened to them on the subway, and came back the next day *unstoppable!*

8. **Be positive with clients today.** As a colleague often tells me, clients can "read and see your attitude before they hear your words."

9. **Talk to yourself.** Brian Tracy, who has studied and spoken on the subject of success, says that salespeople can improve their performance dramatically by simply repeating, "I like myself, I love my work," before each client call. He also says that 95% of emotions depend on how you talk to yourself.

10. **Think how**. When 350,000 salespeople were asked what they thought about during the course of a day, most of them said bills, problems with orders, or worries about that day's sales. The top 10% were thinking about their goals and how to reach them. If you think about what you don't want, such as problems and worries, then you can be sure you'll attract problems and worries to you like iron filings to a magnet. However, if you think about what you want and how to get it, you've just increased the odds of achieving your heart's desire by 100%.

The world is full of people who are doing the things that failures do and expecting to get the things that successful

people get. When it doesn't work, they blame other people, the market, or circumstances.
—Brian Tracy

12

'B' Is for Books

Those who do not read are no better off than those who cannot.
—Chinese Proverb

Some of America's best folklore concerns Abraham Lincoln and how he overcame great hurdles to educate himself. He would walk miles to borrow a book that he hadn't yet read. He read law books at night—by candlelight—after his daily work was done. Yet how many of us have a bookcase just across the room, teeming with books that we haven't touched?

When totalitarian regimes come into power, the first thing they often do is ban or even burn certain books. Why? Because books are powerful! Remember the science-fiction novel *Fahrenheit 451* by Ray Bradbury? The title refers to the temperature at which books burn. Here we sit, with access to more books than any other civilization in the history of the world—yet we usually don't take advantage of these resources.

PICK UP A BOOK

We've never had more access to books than we do now—mega-bookstores, online booksellers, online book excerpts, books to borrow, books to loan, books to read again, audio-books, e-books. And don't forget public libraries. My friend Paul's father swore that he owed his success in life to the robber barons—people like Andrew Carnegie who built public libraries. With only modest means and little formal education, Paul's father educated himself at the library. He built a successful business and raised two sons, each of whom were Rhodes scholars and Harvard graduates—one in law and one in medicine.

Brian Tracy, sales trainer extraordinaire, claims that you can double your income by reading for 30 minutes a day in your field. Tracy tells the story of one sales professional who tried it for six months, and indeed doubled his income. His wife was amazed. She asked him what would happen if he read for an hour every day, and he puzzled, "I don't know!" He tried it and doubled his income again! If you read for an hour a day, you will be covering the equivalent of one book per week, or 52 books per year.

What books should you consider? Well, in addition to books about investing, check these out:

- *See You at the Top* by Zig Ziglar. A modern classic in motivation. Lose that "stinkin' thinkin'!"

- *The Greatest Salesman in the World* by Og Mandino. Set in the ancient Middle East, Mandino's story clarifies the principles used by great salespeople.

- *How I Raised Myself From Failure to Success in Selling*

by Frank Bettger. This book must be 70 years old by now, written by a former professional baseball player, but it still rings true. Even if you're a success, you'll learn from it.

- *The 80/20 Principle* by Richard Koch. The year I first read it, it was the best book I read that year. Also the second best book I read that year (read it twice). Find out why 20% of the things you do produce 80% of the results. Then find out how to do more of them.

- *Healing Back Pain* by Dr. John Sarno. Most top advisors I know have suffered from back pain. Dr. Sarno, who has successfully treated John Stossel (ABC News and Fox Business News), Rosie O'Donnell's producer, and many others, offers some preventative and restorative advice.

- *The New Art of Selling Intangibles* by Donald Korn and LeRoy Gross. An updated version of the 1980s classic, this book continues to help advisors embrace their inner salesperson!

- *The Meditations of Marcus Aurelius.* Really, really, a classic. An ancient Roman classic.

- *The Edge* by Howard E. Ferguson. Written by a champion high-school wrestling coach, this book provides pictures and quotes from athletes and others on subjects such as perseverance and attitude. This one is out of print, so if you can find it, hold on to it!

- *The Magic of Thinking Big* by David J. Schwartz. Are you thinking too small?

- *Think and Grow Rich* by Napoleon Hill. More millionaires attribute their wealth to this book than any other.

- *The Millionaire Next Door* by Thomas J. Stanley. Develop the mindset of a millionaire.

- *The Excellent Investment Advisor* by Nick Murray. Pick this one or any other Murray book. One of the best speakers and writers in our industry.

- *The E-Myth Revisited* by Michael Gerber. Gerber successfully pinpoints a mindset that allows a tiny minority of entrepreneurs to be successful.

- *The 7 Habits of Highly Effective People* by Stephen Covey. Be effective in all parts of your life.

- *Time Power* by Charles Hobbs. I met Hyrum Smith when he was a seminar leader for Charles Hobbs' company—a month before he began FranklinCovey. Smith built a $500-million company teaching the ideas in this book.

In five years you'll be the same person you are now except for the people you meet and the books you read.
—Charlie "Tremendous" Jones, *motivational speaker*

13

'C' Is for Contacts

The best attitude, informed by the best books, is useless if you don't leverage it to contact clients and prospects. Financial advisors who make a consistently large number of contacts seem to have fewer problems—and less time to worry about them—than advisors with low contact numbers.

In fact, if I were to temporarily lose control of my faculties and leave my financial advisor position—the most perfect job in the history of mankind—to become a branch manager, I would make it a rule to delay talking to any advisor about any concern, until that advisor had hit his contact goal for the day. This means that he would have to set such a goal, and that I would have to know about it.

4...3...2...1...CONTACT!

After years of studying big hitters, Phil Broyles, founder of Top Producer, has concluded that successful producers do four things:

- Contact 25 people a day by phone.
- Ask for 12 commitments.
- Ask for three referrals a day.

- Hold two in-person appointments a week.

To hit these kinds of numbers, you'll have to develop a daily game plan. After all, this is a "contact sport." Here are some steps you can take to drive up your contact rate:

- **Whom should we contact?** Clients, prospects, and centers of influence. We should return calls from people who call us and implement a proactive plan for reaching everyone regularly. In our client surveys, most people inform us that they like to hear from their advisor about once a month.

- **How should we contact people?** Primarily by phone. But you can also contact them in person, or by e-mail, letter, or a note attached to a brochure or article. Or ask someone who works with you to call.

- **What kind of system should we use?** I can list on the fingers of one hand the improvements that have increased my business substantially and for a sustained period over the years. One of the most important improvements was the long-ago purchase of a contact management program and a set of audiotapes describing how a successful financial advisor used that system. Here are what those tapes defined as the benefits of an ideal contact management system:

  1. Your computer keeps a record of each contact and dials for you, so you don't have to punch in the phone numbers.

  2. Your program tracks and tallies your contacts, and also provides a history of mailings and other contacts to clients.

3. You can sort people by categories, as well as flag certain individuals for specific reasons (municipal bond buyers, retired people, people you haven't contacted in the past three months, people who attended a recent seminar).

4. You can do mailings and campaigns to people sorted by the categories you determine.

5. You can use preformatted letters, such as thank-you's, appointment confirmations, etc.

6. You can write "quick-letters"—pre-formatted letters that pop up with room for a couple of sentences, such as: "I tried to call you, but couldn't reach you today. Please call me about XYZ."

7. You can set up specific, regular contact schedules using a tickler system. You can also activate one-time notices reminding you to call someone, say, a week before her CD comes due.

8. You can record notes about each contact. I can't tell you what a relief it is not to have to remember that Mary Johnson only buys A-rated or better municipals, or that Bob Stebbens has a high-pitched voice, so don't make the mistake of thinking it's Mrs. Stebbens (true story!). You won't lose clients, and your mind won't have to retain them.

How many people should we contact? This depends upon your seniority and your style. "My business coach and I argue about this one," says one advisor. "He says that the number doesn't matter. I say that I have to get 20 contacts a day as a matter of discipline." Twenty calls a day can be difficult, since some calls last for 30 minutes or more. Other calls might require an hour or so of preparation In your first couple of years, 100 contacts a day is not unreasonable (get those "nos" out of the way to get to the "yeses"). More often than not, the last two to three contacts you make are the most valuable of the day. They may be the hardest people to reach, but they are also the most productive.

And if all that isn't enough to get you started, here's some motivational advice offered by top producers:

- "Make 20 contacts a day, every day, to anybody, and you'll be successful."

- "You better call them, because they're not going to call you."

- "Go out and play in traffic. Good things will happen."

- "Get 20 calls in by noon, 10 by 10 a.m."

Above all, make contact!

14

'D' Is for Discipline

Here's a little story about Dave, a veteran financial advisor, and the investment discipline he uses with clients. This story is intended not to showcase a specific strategy, but rather to outline the benefits of having a discipline.

Early in his career, Dave tried a number of different systems for buying stocks, just as we all have. He tried analyst recommendations, low P/E stocks, high P/E stocks—even letting clients buy hot stocks being hyped in the media. Needless to say, his results were less than stellar.

At a certain point, however, Dave began to notice that one of his clients consistently achieved higher results than the others. This same client displayed a distinct equanimity and calm; he wished all of his clients would maintain such unflappable demeanors.

In an effort to discover the secret behind this client's success, Dave asked him if he would be willing to share his investment philosophy. An orthopedic surgeon and an obviously bright fellow—he had graduated from Williams College with the highest grade point average in 20 years—Dr. H. was only too happy to oblige. He described his system for investing as follows:

I learned most of what I know about investing from my father, incorporating my own real world experience into his philosophy. Here is my thinking:

1. *Over time, stocks perform better than bonds, and bonds perform better than cash.*

2. *The U.S. stock market is relatively efficient. With millions of people looking at every stock, I am unlikely to do substantially better than everyone else via superior stock picking. I would have to pick a company that would not only do well; it would have to do better than other people expect.*

3. *Over time, the stocks of smaller companies tend to do better than the stocks of larger companies. That's logical, because they demand a higher risk/return premium.*

4. *The world is very random. In my medical practice, I have sometimes performed an incredibly intricate arthroscopic surgery extremely well, only to find that the patient's knee doesn't recover 100%. And at other times, I have performed a merely acceptable procedure, yet the patient has experienced a full recovery. Sometimes stocks that look good will tank, while others will perform out of all proportion to reasonable expectations at the outset.*

5. *The stock market only returns 7–9% more than inflation over time, and I'm reluctant to give up much of that profit in fees or costs. Therefore, I don't trade very often. I'm not worried about commissions; I'm concerned about two other costs that can be much higher: taxes and the bid/ask spread on certain stocks. I try never to*

*pay any taxes on my investments. I never sell for a gain in
my taxable accounts unless I can match it up with a loss.
I carry a very small amount of margin—just enough to
match the margin interest against my stock dividends.*

6. *I use Value Line as a guide to selecting my stocks,
because it has a 45-year record of good performance. I
could just as easily use another service, like S&P, but this
one works for me. I buy the stocks they rank 1 (out of 5)
for timeliness.*

A DOSE OF DAVE'S DISCIPLINE

After reflecting on Dr. H.'s approach, Dave decided to develop a very simple investment discipline that now takes
him about 30 minutes a week to administer. Dave's discipline
consists of the following:

1. He educates clients about asset allocation, efficient
   market theory, and his strategy. As a result, he never
   engages in conversations about Intel's whisper earnings or the futures trading in Light Sweet Crude Oil.

2. After setting an asset allocation, he invests in at least
   8–10 stocks that Value Line has ranked 1 (their top
   5%), diversified by industry.

3. He sells stocks when Value Line marks them down to
   a 3. This is a compromise between Value Line's advice
   (sell when stocks move to a 2), and Dr. H.'s approach
   (don't sell unless you need to match a loss with a gain).

4. He only fine-tunes his strategy to diversify by industry
   or to match tax losses with gains. And he doesn't try to
   find corroborating opinions on the stocks he buys. His

reasoning: The more sources that agree with you, the more likely the stocks in question are overvalued. A consensus of opinions does not indicate a great buy.

Since leveraging his solid sell discipline, Dave has become happy and relaxed. By explaining his simple investment philosophy to clients, he teaches them to avoid impulsively selling winners on the rise or stubbornly holding onto losers. Some of his stocks go down, most track the market, and a few really shoot the lights out. But because he never over-promises to clients, they seldom call him to complain—regardless of performance. This allows him to spend more time improving client service and handling referrals, rather than telling stories about individual stocks.

Dave's system may not be perfect, but it works. And no clients have left him to use Value Line on their own. They understand that, without his guidance, they'd be tempted to stray from the straight and narrow.

Generally, Dave's only disagreements are with other financial advisors, who give him a hard time because he doesn't have any opinions on individual companies. Dave just smiles and goes home early.

15

'E' Is for Excel

Before I lose those of you without a slide rule and pocket protector, let me hasten to explain that we're not going to talk about numbers and computations. Instead, we'll look at a few creative but simple ways Excel can help you manage your goals and clients. (If you are under 30, you'll probably know even better and quicker ways to use Excel or other spreadsheets.)

MANAGE YOUR GOALS AND TASKS

Set up five columns with the following labels: Goal, Category, Time Frame, Priority, and Results. Now, start entering information on your goals. Why does this beat writing them on a legal pad or in an MS Word document? Because in Excel, you can sort and rank your goals however you choose.

To sort, highlight the title of the column you've identified as the sorting criterion (Priority, for example). Then go to the top toolbar and select Data Sort, and choose Ascending or Descending. The software will rearrange your spreadsheet accordingly.

This feature allows you to sort using up to three columns. In the spreadsheet, you might sort according to your monthly goals, your business goals, or your "A" goals. You can also change or rearrange the spreadsheet constantly—a practical function not available in other time or task management programs.

MANAGE YOUR CLIENTS

Download your client household information into a spreadsheet, with column headings something like the following: Name, Assets, 12 Mo. Rev., Normal Rev, Rank, Poss. Biz, Poss. Biz $. (You can add more later if you like.) If your firm doesn't have a way to do this, have someone enter it for you. Do this either for all your clients or for the top 100 or so.

In the 12 Mo. Rev. column, you should have the total revenues generated in the past 12 months for the household. Copy that column into Normal Rev., then check through and make any necessary adjustments to make this column the normalized annual revenue. For example, a client who normally pays you about $2,000 per year may have done $20,000 last year because of a property sale. Adjust your records by replacing the figure in the Normal Rev. column. Also, if you have significant business that doesn't show up in transactions—trailers on large mutual fund or money market positions, for example—adjust for that.

Use the Rank column for clients' "importance" ratings, ranked according to a scale such as 1–10 or A–Z. The Possible Biz and Possible Biz $ columns help you estimate future business, and may be empty for many clients.

If you need more room for all your data, widen the columns by moving your cursor to the shaded areas—labeled "A," "B," "C," and so on—at the very top of your spreadsheet.

When you run your mouse over these shaded areas, you'll see the cursor change to a crosshatch with arrows pointing east and west. Click on the line between the columns, drag it to the right, and your columns will grow wider.

It took me about three hours to enter data for my top 230 clients, but the resulting benefits have proven well worth the time. You'll be able to sort and select your clients by every imaginable category, adding columns for telephone numbers, preferred investment types, and other specific information. And you'll have a great system for maintaining your focus on those clients who are the most important to you and your business.

USE SPREADSHEETS EFFECTIVELY

Using these spreadsheets regularly will help you develop a daily game plan and stay focused on priorities. Here are some ideas on how and when to use Excel effectively:

- Print your possible business list every day.

- Review your biggest and best clients every few weeks to ensure that they're receiving excellent service.

- Identify clients who might do more business if you spent more time with them.

- Print your goals and tasks each day, sorted by priority.

Your firm's systems can provide a lot of information. With only a little extra work, however, you can tailor this accurate, powerful program to fit your particular needs. You'll be in command of a tool that will help you be as effective as you possibly can be—every day. If you have any thoughts on how to use Excel to help you manage your business, please send them my way at encouragemen@gmail.com. I'd be interested in any other ideas you have.

16

'F' Is for 'Frequency' (The Movie)

"Frequency" is a great movie about a father who dies fighting a fire when his son is just a boy. As an adult, the son re-connects with his father—across 30 years of time—via Dad's old short-wave radio. By warning his father about the fire, the son helps the father avoid its potentially lethal consequences. By changing history, however, father and son also alter the course of the future. Dad's survival has unexpected implications that must be addressed by both father and son.

The film offers a comic angle on the stock market: at one point the adult son instructs his childhood friend to "remember this one word: 'Yahoo.'" But the principal point is that looking forward and taking steps to intervene in what seems inevitable can impact the future—and help you achieve your long-term goals.

POSTMARKED...ME

Pretend you received a letter from your future self, describing the consequences of your actions. How big-picture motivating would that be?

April 25, 20–:

Dear Me:

I just wanted to list a number of things you've accomplished over the past 30 years. Perhaps a little advance knowledge of your future successes will reassure you that you are on the right track. Here's a preview of your achievements to keep you motivated and moving forward:

Your clients: By guiding people correctly, you have helped hundreds of your clients send their kids to college, receive a better income at retirement—even enjoy a little more fun and less worry. Remember Mr. and Mrs. Stephens? Without you, they would have done business with a guy who would have put them in poorly performing investments, causing them to retire with one-third less money.

New accounts: Remember when you stayed late and opened that $200,000 account for Mr. Johnson, figuring it would generate about $2,000 per year in revenue? Well it did. But you know what else? That account grew 10% per year and now has grown to $3,400,000 for Mr. Johnson, generates $34,000 annually in business, which has totalled much more than $200,000. And because of your good work, Mr. Johnson gave you 14 referrals over the years, most of whom turned into excellent clients. His lifetime value as a client has been enormous. Way to go!

Deferred compensation: I know you realized that your firm's savings plan was a good opportunity when you first saw it. But if only you had known how good. I remember how you ran the calculations on your 401(k) and other plans and discovered that if you kept your business growing—putting the maximum amount into the plan—you would ultimately be among your own wealthiest clients. Contributing 25% was a stretch that first year or two, but you made up your mind to increase production enough to do it, and smiled every year. Thanks.

Contacts and service: Your decision to make one extra contact every day before leaving led to a compounding increase in new accounts. Now—although you haven't always kept track—about 30% of your business derives from those "extra" calls. Another 20% are clients who stayed with you because you gave them excellent service. You never knew it, but when other financial people tried to acquire their business, these clients remembered your efforts to prepare an effective plan for them, always make time for them, and genuinely understand and address their needs. They stayed with us.

Random acts of kindness: Because of the time you spent volunteering for literacy, you saw eight kids go to college who would otherwise have dropped out of high school. Your efforts assisting that Girl Scout troop helped dozens of girls grow up into young women with high self-esteem and a diverse array of accomplishments. Many of those women are now, in turn, helping others. And the three to four times a week you sent notes of appreciation turned into a veritable mountain of goodwill.

Friends: Since you're not overly outgoing, I know that joining the Rotary Club to meet new people felt forced and uncomfortable. But four of my best current friendships sprang from those meetings. My life would be much less interesting without them.

Fitness: Hey, all I need to tell you is that your decision to start exercising and eating right 30 years ago (as I see it, or today as you see it) enabled me to be here today and write this note to you.

Hope this helps. Enjoy the ride, and—to show you my appreciation—I suggest that you skip the dinner salad in Cancun on your trip this summer.

Sincerely,

Me (You)

17

'G' Is for Game

Top producers are competitors. They are corporate athletes and gladiators. They take investment performance and client service very seriously, but they consider it part of the game. They revel in the fact that each day starts with a zero score and has the possibility of being a great day—maybe even a personal record.

MONDAY IS THE BEST DAY—HONEST!

Top producers don't understand why, on Monday mornings, people ask, "How was your weekend?" To them, this is like approaching an NFL player right before the game and asking, "How was your week?" Huh? While top producers can certainly remember what they did last weekend, they're not thinking about it once the workday begins. On Monday mornings, they're wearing their game face; the competition has already started, and the other team is kicking off. Their lives are focused on each day: scoring points and running up the score. They exist in the present. Top producers live for the game, not for the time off.

THE RISK OF LOSING

Top producers love the uncertainty of each new day. They love pitting their skills against the best that the competition can throw at them. Even in their spare time, they would rather watch or compete in a game, because the outcome is yet to be determined. They don't understand why someone would watch "The Wedding Singer" more than once. They were pretty sure the first time that Drew Barrymore was going to marry Adam Sandler. Won't the same thing happen next time?

I'M THE "I" IN TEAM

Top producers work with a team, but understand that they alone are responsible for putting points on the scoreboard. They recognize that each period of the game is important, yet the game is never won until the final period. They often rely on a coach, yet they know that the coach doesn't go out on the field with them. They don't worry about office politics, because they realize that worrying won't help them put points on the scoreboard. With the exception of their clients, they don't care who likes them or who doesn't. They know that practice doesn't make perfect, but that perfect practice makes perfect.

RULES ARE MADE TO BE KEPT

Top producers follow the rules; in fact, they memorize them. They're puzzled when the rules change partway through the game. They're annoyed when they're asked to meet more requirements than the other team. They become apoplectic when they lose game time to fill out paperwork on the sidelines, even if the paperwork is necessary.

THE REAL EQUIPMENT

Top producers look for the best equipment (products and platforms), yet find it humorous that the bat, ball, helmet, and stick manufacturers sometimes think the game is about the equipment they make (think investment products and money managers). Although outside conditions may change—from sweltering heat to blizzard, from bear market to raging bull— top producers keep competing. They know that the final score of the game is determined by their in-house equipment: the heart and brain.

ARE YOU GAME?

Ultimately, top producers know that they are responsible for their own results. They attack with their strengths. They shore up their weaknesses. They discover the current situation's weaknesses and capitalize on them. They know that the purpose of the game is not "to look good" as you strike out. They'll never grimace and grab their leg with a hamstring pull after the opposing running back has made it past them to score a touchdown, what author and speaker Zig Ziglar calls the "loser's limp." Top producers will win ugly, if necessary. But they'll win. And they'll win again tomorrow, too.

18

'H' Is for Hicks

Sol Hicks, a longtime agent at a major insurance company, and once my agent, retired a few years ago. His amazing tale of overcoming adverse circumstances offers valuable lessons for all of us—particularly those hit hard by outside circumstances.

The story of Hicks begins humbly; the son of a cook, he was born in Eufaula, Alabama. Hicks later moved to San Diego, where he built much of his business, but maintained customers in Alabama, as well as in Chicago and throughout the country.

A dedicated agent, Hicks was soon featured in company brochures and frequently recognized as the company's top-performing African-American agent. Despite his successes, Hicks never quite reached the number one overall slot. But even getting close was no small feat, given the 18,000 agents in his division.

Then, Hicks experienced a number of unanticipated setbacks. A car accident left him debilitated; suffering severe, chronic, back pain, he left work on short-term disability. Meanwhile, in Alabama, an aggressive attorney involved in a number of class action suits decided to sue Hick's insurance company through one of Hicks' policyholders. Through no fault of his own, Hicks was forced to spend a great deal of time in court. His productivity dropped substantially, and at one point he was put on probation.

APPROACHING A NEW APPROACH

In Hicks' shoes, a lesser individual might have become discouraged. However, Hicks became more determined than ever to become the number one agent in his company. Leveraging a new approach, he began to talk to friends and clients about his mission to rise to the top, and then asked for their help. A number of them bought into his vision and began to introduce him to others.

Hicks met with individuals, but mostly in small group settings. He spoke in churches, businesses, and homes. He met with business people and professional athletes. He flew all over the country, transacting business wherever he could create it.

In the last two weeks of the year, Hicks found himself in second place. Despite an outstanding year, his production totaled only about half of the top producer's. Someone else might have given up. Instead, Hicks made one more trip, this time to New York to meet with clients trying—ultimately successfully—to take their company public. Hicks sold them as much in those last two weeks as he had in the initial 50 weeks combined. He finished the year in first place.

Hicks held onto his number one position for two more years. He now owns three of the sports coats awarded annually to the insurance company's top agent, like golf's Master's Tournament. What can advisors learn from his experiences?

1. **Think big.** Coming back from disability, court problems, and low production, Hicks didn't simply aim to do well; he wanted to reach the top. He set his sights on becoming the number one agent in the company, and he worked hard to make his dream come true.

2. **Leverage yourself.** An average agent would have spent his time talking with prospects one-on-one. Hicks decided he needed to speak to small groups in order to hit his goals.

3. **Focus on the goal, not the obstacles.** No one would have blamed Hicks for using his back pain, the time he spent on lawsuits, or his firm's insensitivity to rationalize low productivity. But Hicks didn't look for excuses; he looked for new business.

4. **Be a leader.** Hicks wasn't bashful about his vision. He convinced friends and colleagues that he was on a mission, and that they should join him. His vision was so enticing that other people volunteered to help him achieve his goals.

5. **Finish strong.** Hicks could have given up and taken off for the holidays like most other agents. Instead, he persevered and won a big account. Imagine doing half your business in the last two weeks of the year!

You probably have some amazing stories as well. If you know someone who has overcome great obstacles—or have done so yourself—send me an e-mail at encouragemen@ gmail.com. I'd like to hear from you.

19

'I' Is for Illustrate

You know you're listening to a dynamic speaker if she illustrates her message using stories and examples. A boring presenter, on the other hand, may never get his point across, lacking the necessary showmanship to drive his message home. Stories, examples, and analogies convey a wealth of information to an audience; they can make a point, soften a blow, or reinforce a concept. Illustrations help people become emotionally involved, grasp new ideas, and relate intangible investment theories to concrete, real-life objects.

Phil Gramm, former United States senator from Texas, is famous for using anecdotes to hammer his points home. Drawing on the real-life experiences of his constituents, Gramm couches his messages in stories like: "Before I vote to spend more money, I think about Fred Johnson, back in Texas. Fred is a school custodian and is raising four children. I ask myself: 'Is it worth taking Fred's money for this program?'"

A former economics professor, Senator Gramm could certainly wax eloquent about tax policy or supply-side economics if need be. But Gramm realizes that the rhetorical power of a story far outweighs that of a lengthy, fact-riddled lecture. These days, many politicians are taking the concept of "illustration" a step further; they invite the heroes of their stories to appear on stage, relaying their narratives directly to the audience—and providing compelling in-person illustrations of specific political messages.

PAINTING A PICTURE

How can we leverage the power of illustration in our day-to-day activities? Illustration helps us convey ideas in simple terms, stripped of hard-to-grasp theoretical or industry jargon that leaves clients bewildered—and sometimes vexed. Here are some situations where I've seen top producers use good illustrations to drive their message home:

- **To reassure clients that you are as conservative as they are.** "Mrs. Jones, I'm conservative. Some days I wear a belt *and* suspenders! To quote Will Rogers, 'I'm more concerned with the return *of* my money than the return *on* my money.'"

- **To dispense reality to the client seeking a perfect investment.** "Picture this. You have an orange, which contains eight ounces of juice. You have four juice glasses, each of which holds four ounces. Let's call the four juice glasses Safety, Growth, Tax Savings, and Liquidity. Now, you can put four ounces in the Safety glass and four ounces in the Liquidity glass by using a money market fund. Or, using individual growth stocks, you can put four ounces in Growth and two ounces each in Tax Savings and Liquidity. But whatever you do, there's only so much juice in the orange."

- **To convince a client not to sell:** "Mr. Chettle, do you think the value of your house is up or down? Are you going to put it up for sale? Why not? Because it really doesn't matter whether it's up or down in value. You bought it for what it does for you. The roof protects you from the rain, the water heater gives you hot water, and the windows let you look out on the view. Just like your house, the investments we made will help you meet your financial goals, just as we planned. Warren Buffett once suggested that the reason so many people make money on their homes is that they don't get a monthly statement in the mail showing the market value!"

- **To stop a client from chasing performance.** My all-star advisor friend Rick De Soto says, "Mrs. Reinhardt, I don't know if interest rates are going up or down. But recently, I was talking with a longtime client of mine, who said, 'You know, Rick, I've bought tax-free bonds at 12%, and I've bought them at 4%. I can never tell if interest rates are going up or down, so I just invest when I have the money. Overall, I seem to average a pretty good rate.'"

If you're Alan Greenspan testifying before Congress, you can count on your listeners parsing your every word; you won't need stories and examples to capture their attention. But for the rest of us, using illustrations rather than statistics or dry industry terminology helps pique the interest of clients and prospects—and drives our message home.

20

'J' Is for Joke

Having a few jokes at hand is one of the best ways to illustrate a point and endear yourself to clients, prospects, and even colleagues and friends. If you're quick with an anecdote or quip, you'll find yourself better able to navigate through a variety of awkward social situations. A humorous story—or even a charming one-liner—can help you break the ice, neutralize a negative perception, deflect criticism, and relieve tension.

WHY THE LONG FACE?

Suppose a client is complaining about the market being down. Boring advisors will react by yanking out their Ibbotson charts and talking about standard deviation or some other left-brain activity.

Top producers, on the other hand, will be more apt to defuse the situation by adopting an emotional, intuitive, and even humorous approach. Confident in their abilities, they may offer a response like: "Some days you're the windshield; some days you're the bug," or even, "Some days you eat the bear; some days the bear eats you." While you should be careful not to appear too flip, a right-brain connection, coupled with a confident delivery, will help you make your point loud and clear.

THE JOKE'S ON ME!

Self-effacing humor is particularly effective for relaxing a crowd and neutralizing negative perceptions about you and your work. During the 2000 presidential elections, for example, both Al Gore and George W. Bush used humor to great effect at the annual Al Smith dinner. Gore, responding to criticism that he is too detail-oriented, stated: "I'm using 43.2% fewer statistics in each speech now." Bush, on the other hand, played off his "not-so-smart" media image by comparing himself to William F. Buckley, a well-known intellectual in attendance at the event. Bush quipped, "Bill Buckley and I have a lot in common. While at Yale, he wrote a book. While at Yale, I read one."

TWO ADVISORS WALK INTO A BAR...

Jokes can also help you break the ice in more general social situations where you're aiming to work the room. You should always consider your audience and your timing, but in general, a well-delivered anecdote tends to cultivate amiable feelings, encouraging your listeners to become more relaxed and open to your ideas.

Here are a few examples of stories I've heard financial advisors tell about themselves and the industry:

ABRAHAM LINCOLN

We had just finished a particular transaction when a client said, "Joe, you remind me of Abraham Lincoln." Flattered, I inquired, "Is it because I'm tall and have a beard?" "No," she replied. "Is it because of my obvious sense of integrity?" "No, that's not it either," she answered. "Well, why do I remind you of Lincoln, then?" "Because as far as we know, he didn't know a darn thing about stocks either!"

HEAD HOG

One day when my assistant answered the phone, the voice on the other end said, in a deep Texas accent, "Could I speak to the head hog at the trough?" Slightly offended, my assistant replied, "Sir, I'm not sure who you mean." He answered, "Just put me through to the head hog at the trough." She said, "Sir, Mr. Byers is a professional financial advisor, and I don't believe that he would appreciate being referred to in that way. I believe I'm going to hang up now—" But before she finished, he interrupted, "Ma'am, I'm sorry if I offended you, but I just sold my ranch and I have two million dollars to invest. I want to talk to the head hog at the trough." Being well trained, she made a hasty recovery, coming back with, "Hold on, I think I see the big pig coming right now!"

NEW ZEALAND VACATION

A stockbroker went on vacation to New Zealand. Driving along a country road one day, he stopped as he came up on a herd of sheep. He waited for them to cross, and got out of his car to talk to the shepherd a moment. "Are you a gambling man?" he asked the shepherd. "I suppose so. Why do you ask?" "Well," the broker replied, "If I could guess the exact number of sheep you have, could I have one?" The shepherd thought a minute, and replied, "Sure." The broker said, "273." "You're right," said the amazed shepherd. So the broker made his pick and put it in the car.

As he started to drive off, the shepherd knocked on his window. "Would you like to make another bet?" "I suppose so," said the broker. "If I can guess your profession, can I have my sheep back?" the shepherd asked. The broker figured that was a pretty safe bet, since he was 10,000 miles from home, so he agreed. "You're a stockbroker, aren't you?" Astounded, the broker admitted that he was. "But how did you know?" he asked. As he took the animal back, the shepherd explained, "Because with 273 sheep to choose from, you picked the dog!"

Remember: Be Funny; Make Money!

21

'K' Is for Kaput

Have you ever seen a car sitting on blocks in someone's yard? That's "kaput," which comes from a German word meaning "broken." Until it's fixed, the car is little more than an eyesore—whether it's a '78 Pinto or last year's Lexus.

Now think about your business. Has some element of your practice gone kaput—without you even realizing it? As we move into the rest of this year, take stock of your business efforts. Review the following areas to identify what's working—and what's kaput:

- **Merchandising.** Are you responding to calls from clients? Are you systematically making enough outgoing calls and recommending investments?

- **Prospecting.** Do you set aside time every day—without fail—to talk to new people about what you do and how you can help them? How many people do you talk to and when? And if you are having trouble making these calls, do you seek out motivational support—listening to Dr. Aaron Hemsley's CD's, for example, or reading Nick Murray's chapter on call reluctance?

- **Motivation.** Are you culling inspiration daily, or simply waiting for a spark? Are you learning from the hundreds of thousands of professionals, salespeople, and leaders who have faced—and overcome—the same difficulties you encounter?

- **Knowledge.** Have you studied the new IRA distribution rules? Have you watched the tax videos to get up to date? Have you looked at how other people invest their money for ideas on new ways to help your clients?

- **Goals.** Where is that business plan you wrote in December? Have you revised your plan to deal with the reality of the moment, rather than with outdated forecasts or projected figures?

- **Shape.** How are you faring physically, emotionally, and spiritually? Have you lost track of what is really important in life? Do you need to get back to what matters most?

- **Support.** Have you gone into a shell, or are you sharing ideas with other successful financial advisors? Can you offer each other encouragement?

DON'T CAVE IN TO KAPUT

Let's face it: there's a measure of consolation in staying kaput. First, you don't have to exert any effort. Sometimes it's easier to keep your car on blocks than to get outside and peer under the hood. Second, never fixing the car means never driving it—and never facing the possibility of a wreck (rejection) or getting lost (making mistakes). Third, your car looks pretty good out there, and the radio still works. What's the big deal?

But your car—and, more important, your business—won't function smoothly until you have identified what's kaput and fixed it. A little effort now will pay off in the long run. Get your car and your business running—and out on the road.

22

'L' Is for Level

In general, we can break down each of our business activities into three broad levels of operation: mission, strategy, and product. And this breakdown holds true generally—whether we are playing a sport, hosting a dinner, or building our business. Consider the table below:

Levels	Our Business	Sports	Cooking
Level I	What business am I in? (Money manager, stockbroker, financial planner?)	What game do I play? (Football, rugby, or baseball?)	What do I cook? (Casserole, cake, full meal, breakfast?)
Level II	How do I do it? (Strategy, tactics, calls, financial plans, time management, etc.)	How do I play it? (Rules, equipment, practice, teammates, position, etc.)	How do I prepare it? (Recipe, ingredients, utensils, oven, time, serving, etc.)
Level III	What product do I use? (XYZ Funds, ABC Manager, or individual stocks?)	What equipment do I use? (Spalding or Rawlings?)	Where do I buy ingredients? (Kroger, Costco, or Safeway?)

Looking over the table, you'll quickly note the importance of Level I to our success. Our definition of who we are—whether we're salesmen, portfolio managers, asset allocators, financial planners, or stock traders—determines the fundamentals: our role and target market.

On the other hand, Level III is of relatively minor importance. It's all about products—which football we push across the goal line or where we buy our flour and eggs. Products don't define our success, but we hear a lot about them—primarily because of their importance to Spaulding, Kroger, and Safeway, not to mention XYZ Funds or ABC asset manager. Products are the very reason these companies exist, and they deploy a host of wholesalers and media to bombard us with their marketing messages.

Level II is where we really play the game. This level determines most of our performance and accounts for the majority of our profits. This is where we should spend 90% of our time, effort, mental energy, and money.

LEVEL WITH YOURSELF

To excel at Level II, we need to be proactive about finding the resources that will help us serve our clients and build our business. We improve our Level II performance when we study IRA distribution rules or new tax strategies, for example, or when we adopt new best practices that fit our businesses, or when we update our knowledge of marketing, selling, merchandising, and time management.

Of course, there are a number of Level III-type companies that can help us improve our Level II performance. They include sales and management consultancy firms like those run by Bill Good, Matt Oechsli, Steve Moeller, Bill Bachrach, Michael Gerber, and many others. And we also have a number of industry resources available, such as our branch managers, our firms' training departments, the office copy of *Registered Representative* magazine—and Horsesmouth.

To measurably improve our performance, we need to start identifying activities that can help us excel at Level II—and building these activities into our daily game plan. As comedienne Lily Tomlin once said, "I always wanted to be somebody, but I should have been more specific." Try these strategies for determining exactly who you want to be—and becoming that individual as quickly as possible:

- **Read.** Consider reading the writing of some excellent management consultants, including W. Timothy Gallwey, Stephen Covey, and Bill Good. You will also find nuggets of wisdom in many of the industry's trade magazines.

- **Listen to audio.** Nightingale-Conant has thousands of CDs and audio books from some of the world's best motivational speakers. Bill Good sells the speeches from top producers at his annual marketing conventions, and at least two mutual fund companies will send you periodic or quarterly tapes containing essential business-building ideas.

- **Gain knowledge.** Explore Horsesmouth and other financial services websites to gain more real-world knowledge of the industry and your clients.

- **Acquire professional credentials.** Consider earning your CFP or CIMA designation.

- **Benchmark your practice.** Visit a top producer once a year or once a quarter to see how she conducts her daily business.

- **Take a time- or life-management course.** Frankin Covey offers a time-management workshop called

"What Matters Most" several times a year in locations all over the country.

- **Prioritize your schedule.** Plan a few minutes every day—and maybe two hours every week—to review your goals, your game plan, and your life.

You and I need to be sure that we know what business we're in and why (Level I), that we're planning and executing the proper strategies (Level II), and that we're not being overwhelmed by other people's investment products, branding, or advertising (Level III). Once we're clear on our operational priorities and can marshal the resources we need, we will spend more of our time where it counts the most—and take our business to a whole new level.

23

'M' Is for Mindset

Nick Murray—one of the finest writers in the industry—has given us some extraordinarily imaginative suggestions for connecting with prospects and building new business. My favorite is his description of the prospecting mindset—a description that could only have been written by a veteran of the industry's trenches and front lines.

In his book, *The Excellent Investment Advisor*, Murray explains why prospecting is problematic and how to overcome its challenges. I've paraphrased his explanation here:

Suppose a rat in a cage is taught to hit a button for food. The rat learns to love to hit the button, receiving a reward each time. Then a less-than-kind psychology professor rewires that button, so that now, each time the rat hits the button, it receives an electric shock. The rat can't quite figure this out, so it keeps going to the button and keeps getting shocked. After a while, the lapses between touches on the button become further and further apart, until finally the rat is cowering in the corner of the cage, slowly starving to death. But at least it's not getting zapped by that button again!

That's a bit like what we run into in this business. People tell us they don't have any money, they don't trust us, they only use no-load funds—they reject us in thousands of ways. We hit the button and get zapped often enough that we decide to do anything rather than be zapped again. So we go for coffee a little more often, study asset allocation, reread *The Wall Street Journal*—and soon enough, our production spirals downward.

But imagine a different scenario. Picture yourself in a beautiful room containing only two items: a comfortable chair situated in front of a slot machine. This is a very special slot machine—for every thousand quarters, it pays off $1,000. You find that you can pull the handle once every 10 seconds.

Pulling that handle will certainly take a lot of work and persistence. With time off to go to lunch and read the *Journal,* you might find that the machine pays off about twice a day. You might even come in a little early the next day, skip the *Journal*, and bring your lunch to devote more time to pulling the handle. With a little extra effort, you might get the machine to pay off three times—a very good day for you.

ANALYZING THE ANALOGY

Is this analogy flawed? Only in its details. No, you can't talk to somebody new every 10 seconds. By the same token, it takes a lot fewer than a thousand people to yield one new prospect. Never mind the mechanics; focus on the great, cosmic law. And realize that, whatever its flaws, this analogy is infinitely closer to reality than the rat in the psychology experiment. In that story, the rat gets zapped every single time until he despairs and dies. In the fable of the elegant machine, almost every try doesn't pay off. And therein lies the supreme secret of our business: the golden "almost!"

PROSPECTING FORMULA

Murray goes on to describe a prospecting formula where "N" equals the number of times you need to insert a quarter to attract one good prospect. To become a prospecting powerhouse, all you have to do is to slowly—but permanently—increase the number of calls you make, or your "N:"

"Almost everybody you ever prospect will decline to do business with you. Every 'N' number of times you hear 'no,' you will hear one 'yes.' Stated algebraically, $P=1/N$. That means that virtually all prospecting calls are good; the only bad prospecting call is the one you didn't make. Success is the inevitable consequence of the failure to fail."

Are you willing to try?

24

'N' Is for Niche

To market your services successfully, you'll need to understand how your prospects think. And the beauty of targeting a specific niche is that you'll study and talk to dozens, maybe hundreds of prospects in the same situation. You'll really become familiar with your prospects' pre-existing mindset—and you can tailor your approach accordingly.

Here's how Les Anderson, author of *You Are the Product,* explains it: If there are 200 competitors with a bond to sell, how many of them can have the very highest rate? Only one, of course. So if you are competing on the basis of highest rate or best performance, then you stand a very small chance of being the best or the highest on any given day.

But suppose you specialize in a niche—let's say ski resort owners. Introducing yourself on your first call, you say, "Mrs. Rossignol, I specialize in working with ski resort owners to help them handle the financial needs that come with uneven cash flow." How many people can say that? Very few, if any. How many people are you competing with now? Probably none. Do you have to come up with the highest rate or the lowest cost? Not at all. Are you even competing? Not really. You are now operating in a monopoly. You've chosen your target market, and you're the only one there.

OCCUPY CLIENTS' "SHELF SPACE"

Here's another example. Try the following exercise:

1. Name a brand of laundry detergent.

2. Name a brand of toothpaste.

According to Anderson, close to 80% of people will reply "Tide" to the first question, and 70% will answer "Crest" to the second question. Both of those are Procter & Gamble (PG) products. If you answered "Tide" and "Crest," you probably did so because P&G owns that product's "shelf space" in your mind. P&G bought it years ago, when you were just a little kid watching television. And P&G owns it, just as surely as you own your 401(k) plan.

What would it take to remove "Tide" from the shelf marked "laundry detergent" in your mind? A lot, when you consider this statistic: Of the 25 leading brands of consumer products in 1921, 20 are still No. 1 today. One slipped to No. 5, and four others moved all the way down to No. 2. And that's after competitors spent hundreds of millions of dollars trying to unseat them.

So if you're the brand manager for another company, what can you do? You can either focus your efforts on moving "Tide" off the shelf (which will never happen) or on creating new shelf space for your product. You might market it as the "eco-friendliest" detergent, or the "blue jean" detergent, or maybe something specifically for laundromats. Whatever it is, by positioning your product into its own special category, you're allowing it to stand alone as a monopoly or a leading brand in that niche.

TARGET AN UNUSUAL NICHE

You can use this same type of marketing to position your financial services. In each prospect's mind, there is a shelf labeled "investments" or "financial advice." And let's face it, for most people in the world, you and I don't occupy that space—although if you're fortunate, your firm's name does. But you need to accept that whoever occupies that shelf space—be it Bank of America, Fidelity, or Joe, their college roommate—is likely to stay there. Rather than try to move them out, your best hope is to create your own category and operate in a monopoly. Here are some examples of financial professionals who have successfully targeted unusual niche markets:

One CPA, an immigrant from Taiwan, developed a practice largely made up of Taiwanese immigrant doctors. But he still wanted some new clients. When, after scanning his book, he noticed that he worked with several doctors from Pakistan, he created another specialty: working with Pakistani physicians. In fact, being Taiwanese had little to do with his first success—but working with a niche of people who shared the same needs and knew each other did. And by cultivating relationships within a specific group of professionals, he was able to expand his business more quickly through referrals.

If you think that niche markets consist only of people with a lot of money, listen to this story. One advisor built a substantial adjunct to his business by becoming an expert at helping people place their loved ones in nursing homes. He'd reorganize their assets to protect them from nursing-home costs and capitalize on Medicaid. At one point, he would regularly receive about a dozen referrals a month, mostly from attorneys who recognized his expertise. And he brought in other business by helping these families rearrange their assets to increase their income or meet other goals.

FOLLOW THESE TIPS

Look around your office. Some of your colleagues are probably significant niche marketers. They may have built their niche by following a few of these tips:

- Define your niche.

- Include fewer than 200 names in each market segment. "Doctors" is much too large a category.

- Skip niches that are too popular—executives at Microsoft, for example, or airline pilots approaching retirement.

- Look for wealthy clients in a small field. I've seen affluent people who own hearing aid stores and Hallmark Card shops, or who sell law books to attorneys.

- Consider overlooked professions like auctioneering, one of the highest-paid careers in the country.

- Visit your local library and look up a directory of associations that can help you find all of the different niches that make up our great economy. Pick a niche—or two or three—and go for it!

25

'O' Is for Opportunity

In Chinese, the word for "opportunity" is made up of two characters: the first character denotes crisis, and the second stands for "what the heck happened to the Nasdaq?" Or something like that. In every market drop, many advisors are quickly immobilized. Others join their ranks as the market reaches new lows. Yet there are plenty of great opportunities that surface when times are hard. Here are 10 trends that work in advisors' favor, and how to take advantage of them:

1. **Money is in motion.** People are definitely open to moving their accounts. There are about 50,000 well-qualified prospects out there for every one of your existing clients, so the odds of signing on some new accounts are definitely in your favor.

2. **Think globally.** We're not limited just to opportunities in the U.S. markets. We, or managers on our behalf, can search the world for opportunities.

3. **Turn growth into income.** If your clients are already loaded up with bonds, look for growth funds with a systematic withdrawal provision. If you look at the bar graphs and tree charts that mutual fund families use in their sales literature, their "$10,000 turning into $2

million" scenarios always begin in times like these.

4. **Put tax laws on your side.** Consider using a systematic withdrawal on a tax-managed growth fund. Run a hypothetical on a tax-managed fund, plug in the applicable tax rates, and see what happens. In an example I ran for myself, the effective tax rate comes out to about 5% over 10 years, with an $800 monthly withdrawal from a $100,000 investment.

5. **Look for bargain hunters.** Believe it or not, there are actually some investors who have been saving cash for a time like this. Find them and help them to understand that now is the time, this is the place, and you are the person they should trust with their money.

6. **Advice has risen in value.** After attending *The Los Angeles Times* Investment Expo after the dot-com bust, a client reported not only that there were fewer attendees, but that the no-load fund companies were gone, the free tote bags were conspicuously absent, and the daytrading trailer all set up with computer terminals to teach people how to invest had vanished. *The Wall Street Journal* even ran an article about how financial services firms are seeing a real jump in the number of new clients and inquiries. All this goes to prove that in tough times, real investors would rather hear from you than talk to someone at the other end of a toll-free number.

7. **Tout your financial conservatism.** One of my colleagues is putting together a letter right now that starts: "You may remember the Barbara Mandrell

song, 'I Was Country When Country Wasn't Cool.'
Well, I was financially conservative when conservative
wasn't cool."

8. **Get back to the basics.** Lay the foundation for years
of future success by revising the tenet of asset allocation and managing expectations. This had to happen
sometime, big guy!

9. **Find the silver lining.** As people in our industry leave,
you will pick up new accounts. These new clients may
come via your branch manager or from friends of your
clients who have lost their advisor to a sudden career
change. Which means that when the market turns,
there will be more business for you. Just ask any 20-
year veteran how bad news often turns into an opportunity in the end.

10. **Be thankful for your good fortune.** Overheard conversation: Young advisor: "I sure hope today is a good
day." Gray-haired veteran: "You live in America. Your
family is healthy. You have a career with unlimited opportunity. You've already won life's lottery! Ninety-nine
percent of the world's population would trade places
with you right now. How can it not be a good day?"

26

'P' Is for Perspective

Not long after the attacks of 9-11, critical stress counselor Dr. Kevin Elko spoke to a group of financial advisors. (In addition to counseling financial professionals, Dr. Elko also speaks to National Football League teams, such as the Dallas Cowboys.) He had just flown in from three days—and 21 meetings—of speaking to and counseling traumatized groups in New York City. Here is what he said that helped put recent events in perspective:

- **Distance yourself from events.** Dr. Elko set a chair on stage and told us, "This is my only visual aid today. This is a chair." He then walked five steps away from the chair. "This is me. I am not the chair. The chair is over there. The tragedy that happened is the chair. The market is the chair. You are not the chair. As I told people 21 times in New York, you are not the tragedy. I'm telling you today that you are not the market. You are separate from the market. You can watch how it acts with interest—even with hurt and pain—but always remember, you are separate and can choose your reaction to it."

- **Choose your emotions.** "Events do not cause your emotions," says Elko. "What you decide to think about events does."

- **Decide what to tell yourself.** Elko talked to Emmitt Smith (the Dallas Cowboys running back) and asked him what was the best game he ever had. Without hesitation, Smith replied, "237 yards against the Philadelphia Eagles." And what was he thinking? "I was just running the ball."

- **Determine what motivates you.** Elko told a story about how the captain of the Czechoslovakian national hockey team motivated his teammates to beat the Russians. The captain wore the number 68 because in 1968, the Soviet Union invaded Czechoslovakia and his grandfather was killed. "The Czech captain gave a talk before they played the Russian team," says Elko. "The game was over after his talk. You know who won. Before you can accomplish something worthwhile with your life, figure out what motivates you. What is your '68'?"

  More on motivation. A very successful financial advisor in the Midwest told Elko how he stayed motivated. He said, "My mother put three kids through Boston University, as a machinist. Two days after she wrote the last check, she died. To me, every one of my clients looks like my mother." What is your '68'?

- **Define success and your approach to it.** "The best thing you can do for America today is to get your motor running," says Elko. "You don't get success. You are success. And your wealth is not money. It's time."

- **Cultivate your relationships.** Elko recounted an interesting study in The New England Journal of Medicine. "People live longer in Rosetta, Pa., than in any other community in the country. Researchers discovered that a lot of them ate red meat every day and even smoked." So why did they live longer? Elko said that they had a front porch. Every day they would sit out on the porch and talk to neighbors who walked by. "It's all about relationships," says Elko.

- **Reaffirm your faith.** Elko reminded us of a Pearl Bailey quote: "We see God every day; we just don't recognize Him."

- **You are not alone.** Sometimes you can find advice in surprising places. It may help you to remember that others have suffered through and overcome similar tragedies. Elko told a humorous story about how one baseball icon helped another get through the inevitable slumps that occur in a professional athlete's career: "After the third time Billy Martin was fired as manager of the New York Yankees, he was replaced by Yogi Berra. When Berra got to his desk, he found two envelopes left for him by Billy Martin. The first one said, 'Open only in case of extreme emergency.' The second one said, 'Open only in case of terrible, dire, extreme emergency.'

"Early on, the Yankees lost six games in a row. Yogi opened the first envelope. The note inside read, 'Blame it all on me.' So he blamed all the team's troubles on Billy Martin. It worked, and took the pressure off him. A month later, the team lost nine games in a row. Yogi opened the second envelope. The note inside read, 'Prepare two envelopes.'"

27

'Q' Is for Quotes

As this is written we end one of the most difficult years in recent history. A few words from the wise about our business, bear markets, and investments might be just what the doctor ordered. Some of the following quotations, I hope, will be old friends. Others may be delightfully new to you:

- *The stock market has forecast eight of the last three recessions.*
  —Paul Samuelson

- *The function of economic forecasting is to make astrology look respectable.*
  —John Kenneth Galbraith

- *When you sell in desperation, you always sell cheap.*
  —Peter Lynch

- *People's investments would be more intelligent if stocks were quoted once a year.*
  —Warren Buffett

- *I have seen many investors dispose of a holding that was to show stupendous gain in the years ahead because of this fear of a coming bear market.*
  —Philip Fisher

- *To buy when others are despondently selling and to sell when others are greedily buying requires the greatest fortitude, even while offering the greatest reward.*
  —Sir John Templeton

- *The time of maximum pessimism is the best time to buy, and the time of maximum optimism is the best time to sell.*
  —Sir John Templeton

- *Far more money has been lost by investors preparing for corrections or trying to anticipate corrections than has been lost in the corrections themselves.*
  —Peter Lynch

- *Buy when there's blood in the streets.*
  —Bernard Baruch

- *Even if it's your own blood.*
  —Corollary by unknown contributor

- *This time, like all times, is a good one, if we but know what to do with it.*
  —Ralph Waldo Emerson

- *My investment advice is simple: Buy a stock. When it doubles, sell it. If it don't double, don't buy it.*
  —Will Rogers

28

'R' Is for Recommit

There are a number of times during the year that seem just right for pausing to re-evaluate where we are in our lives and business. Times like year-end, summertime vacation, just before school starts in the fall, or even just a long week-end. These are all opportunities to breathe deeply and take a new bearing on our future.

Maybe this is a useful time to look around, evaluate your life, and recommit yourself to the important pieces of your life and your work. Do you ever envy students, who get to end one term, then start another with renewed vigor? Or professional athletes, who end one season, however well or poorly, take a break, then begin a new season with spring training, or summer workouts, and have time to recommit themselves to do their best? There is no reason you can't create your own new season, term, or year.

THE SEASON OF RECOMMITTING

As you think about this, maybe it's time to:

- **Recommit yourself to excellence in your personal relationships.** Would your spouse, kids, and other family members feel that you were committed to them? Could they count on you to be there, both physically and mentally, when they need you? Or have the pressures and habits of daily life taken you away from what is really important? It's not too late to recommit yourself to them. To humbly tell them that you're going to do just that can be a great start. Then follow through.

- **Recommit yourself to your clients.** These people put their trust in you. You can't control how investments perform, but neither does that have to stop you from doing all that you can for your clients. What about beginning to call them, and saying, "Mr. Chase, we've been through some tough markets lately, haven't we? I just wanted to call and tell you that I am committed to working with you for the long-term, and that I will do everything possible to help you and your family meet your long-term goals. I'm here with you through thick and thin." Wouldn't you like to hear something like that from your banker, your attorney, your CPA, or your financial advisor?

- **Recommit yourself to your goals.** Suppose you're nearing the end of one term, season, or year. (As an aside, in a football game, more points are scored in the last two minutes of the first half and the last two minutes of the second half than in the other 56 minutes combined, so you still have time!) I've checked the employee handbook at every firm, and there is absolutely no requirement to do the same amount of business next year as you did this year. You make the rules in the goal-setting game!

- **Recommit yourself to work.** Look around your office. If you see someone who has been around for years, you're seeing an advisor who has recovered from seeing the S&P drop by about 50% more than once, then built his or her business back. If you see someone else who started in the business 30 years ago, you're seeing someone who chose to come into this industry at a time when the Dow was around 800, and had been stuck in that range for 10 years.

Yet some of those people are million dollar producers now. And they got there by hard work, by perseverance, and by continuing to bring in new clients and work with their existing clients, day in and day out, no matter what. When the prime interest rate broke 20% and their clients' bonds hit a new low, they recommitted themselves to call more people to ask them to buy more. When the DJIA hit 750 in 1982, they recommitted themselves to prospecting and to bringing in new investors who could become convinced of the great potential of our capital markets. They prepared financial plans, they ran asset allocation strategies for clients, and they worked extra hours to hold seminars and meet new people. They didn't have 30-year track records of stock market performance to fall back on, as you still have. But they had a great product: Themselves and their ability to guide their clients. And they recommitted themselves daily to getting that message across.

You could say it many ways. Renew your successful habits. Revive your business. Regenerate your good attitude. Reinvigorate your life. Restore your character. But whatever words you use, take a little time as you end one season and begin another, to recommit yourself to the life of excellence that you deserve and are intended to have.

29

'S' Is for Survivor

When I was a rookie, I often heard old-timers say: "Survival pays extremely well in this business." But survival isn't always easy to come by. In tough times, people are struggling, failing, and even giving up because they don't believe their efforts will pay off. But successful producers with weighty books will tell you that, in fact, it's during hard times that they actually pick up the most new assets and the largest number of disgruntled investors from other firms. The financial plans and investments you recommend today represent the ties that bind you to your clients in the future.

WHY SURVIVE?

Recently, my wife and I had dinner with one of these top producers, and I asked him for a topic suggestion starting with the letter "S." His response? Survival. "Advisors have to learn how to survive. We need to do the right business now, and not do business for the wrong reasons. I may only do 70% as much business as what I did last year, but that's OK if I'm still doing business according to my plan and doing the right kind of things for my clients."

So, borrowing some analogies from the hit television show "Survivor," let's talk about what it takes to outwit, outplay, and outlast in our business and stay in the running until the final tribal council:

1. **You've embarked on a strange new adventure.** The rules you formerly employed to build your business have changed. Just as "Survivor's" contenders needed to realize that they were in a new environment—a deserted island, the Australian outback, the wilds of Africa—so do you. This territory has the potential to test all of your limitations. The investment world doesn't look the same as it did two years ago; you need to learn how to make it work for you in new and different ways.

2. **Help your tribe.** You can't make it to the end on your own. You need the help of other people—from your manager to your sales assistant to the people in the home office. And when you see others struggling, do what you can to help them, too.

3. **Forge an alliance.** Just as the first "Survivors" formed a coalition of four to protect themselves from being voted off the island, you can form a strategic alliance—you, a CPA, an estate planning attorney, and an insurance agent—that supports and safeguards your clients' future, as well as your own.

4. **It's not about the money.** Your survival is about doing the right things every day—even when you can't see the fruits of your labor. If your solution to a problem gives you inconsistent results, approach it from another angle. Right now, you want to focus on winning the daily challenge and letting advisors from other tribes (OK, firms) get voted off by their clients.

5. **Win the immunity challenges.** Become one of the top 5% who make their daily contacts and initiate and complete their business planning—and get in early. You will be immune to serious production problems. This, in turn, will lead to more and more assets under management, which is really how you win the immunity challenge.

6. **Remember at all times:** "Survival pays well in our business." In the television show, the last survivor wins a million dollars. In our business, you'll not only earn the big bucks; you'll build a career, provide for your family, and earn the respect of clients and colleagues who will admire the way you've played the game.

30

'T' Is for Thanks

At a business convention, a procession of vendors came to the stage to talk about their new products. One by one, they each spent 30 minutes telling some of their best clients about the exciting new developments in the year ahead. The lone exception was the representative from IBM. He came to the stage, looked out at hundreds of his best customers gathered there, and said only six words: "Thank you. Thank you. Thank you."

This story should remind us to periodically thank our clients. But how can we deliver a message that has the same powerful simplicity as the IBM representative's?

SAMPLES OF GRATITUDE

One possible system is to keep track of all the people you have done business with during the week, and send them a thank-you letter. You may start with a few basic letters, which you can rotate every month. Then, once you discover, as I did, that some people seem to call and do more business every time they receive a letter, you could add many others.

Below are four sample thank-you letters that have worked for me. Some I've learned and adapted from industry experts such as Bill Good. Others were generated in my own practice. Feel free to try any of these or create your own. The more you personalize these letters by highlighting, underlining, and adding postscripts (P.S.'s) that are pertinent to you and your client, the better they will be.

Thank-you letter #1

> Dear Mr. Client:
>
> Today I searched through my dictionary for a new word to express my appreciation and gratitude.
>
> My search kept bringing me back to two very traditional words: thank you.
>
> So, Mr. Client, I'll stay with tradition and say: Thank you for your business. I look forward to working with you in the future.
>
> Sincerely,
>
> Your Advisor

Thank-you letter #2

> Dear Ms. Client:
>
> Thank-you for your recent investment business. It is an honor to have a chance to work with you to help you meet your investment goals.
>
> I'm glad that you feel comfortable

enough with me and my service to send me your business. If you know of anyone else we might be able to help, please let me know.

Sincerely,

Your advisor

Thank-you letter #3

Dear Mrs. Valued Client:

Thank you for your investment business. It's always appreciated and valued. I was just reading an article about investment "axioms." Some are old, but some may be new to you:

- "Time will make you a winner."
- "Bears get fat, and bulls get fat, but hogs get slaughtered!"
- "You can't grow an oak tree by digging it up every week."
- "Spend interest, never principal."
- "Never overreach for yield. Remember, more money has been lost searching for yield than at the point of a gun."
- "You cannot eat relative performance."

- "Smart guys don't turn stupid overnight."
- "Trees don't grow to the sky."
- "If you fail to plan, you're planning to fail."

Sincerely,

Your Advisor

Thank-you letter #4

This is my personal favorite:

Dear Mr. Client:

Up in the mountains of California—in a place called Big Bear—there is a convenience store named Triangle Grocery. On the outside of their wall is a sign that reads:

"We're A Convenience Store, 'Cause It's More Convenient For Us If You Shop Here!"

If I may turn that sentiment around a bit, may I say that I hope it's always convenient for you to do business with us here at our firm. Thank you for your investment business and please let me know if we ever fall short. We appreciate you.

Sincerely,

Your Advisor

31

'U' Is for Unstoppable

"Stories of the human spirit, of people who have overcome fear, doubt, and great adversity to achieve what the rest of the world saw only as impossible," is the subject of the book called *Unstoppable*, by Cynthia Kersey. If the 45 stories in this book don't inspire you, then you'd better hold a mirror in front of your mouth to see if it fogs up, because you may not be among the living!

Here's a summary of one of the stories included in this inspiring book. Legson Kayira, a 16-year-old African, set out on the journey of his life with a five-day supply of food, a Bible, *The Pilgrim's Progress*, a small ax for protection, and a blanket. He was going to walk three thousand miles from his tribal village, north across the wilderness of East Africa to Cairo, where he would board a ship to America to get a college education. His dream was to be like his heroes, Abraham Lincoln and Booker T. Washington.

It was 1958. It took him two years to reach Cairo. On his way there, he stopped to work for six months in Kampala, the capital of Uganda. He found a library with a directory of American Colleges. He wrote to Skagit Valley College in Mt. Vernon, Wash. The dean there was so impressed with his determination that he granted him admission, a full scholarship, and a job that would pay him room and board. Yet he still had to get to the United States. Months passed and he finally made it to Cairo. The students at Skagit Valley College sent $650 to cover his airfare to America. He arrived with his two books in hand to enroll. But his education didn't stop with Skagit Valley College. He became a professor of political science at Cambridge University in England, and a respected author. As he summarizes his experience: "I learned I was not, as most Africans believed, the victim of my circumstances, but the master of them."

QUOTES FROM THE MASTERS

You and I don't have to be the victims of the markets or business trends; we can be masters of them. Does any one of us have less food, clothing, or education than Legson Kayira? Yet how many of us can match him in determination? Do you know that there are successful advisors who are blind, deaf, or paraplegics? Are we as unstoppable as they are?

Kersey offers a number of inspiring quotes in her book. Here are a few that resonated with me:

I claim to be no more than an average man with below average capabilities. I have not the shadow of a doubt that any man or woman can achieve what I have if he or she would put forth the same effort and cultivate the same hope and faith.
—Mahatma Gandhi

Make no little plans; they have no magic to stir men's blood. Make big plans. Aim high in hope and work.
—Daniel H. Burnham, *Chicago architect and planner*

There is no failure except in no longer trying. There is no defeat except from within, no really insurmountable barrier save our own inherent weakness of purpose.
—Elbert Hubbard

I am looking for a lot of men who have an infinite capacity to not know what can't be done.
—Henry Ford

I hated every minute of the training, but I said, 'Don't quit. Suffer now and live the rest of your life as a champion.'
—Muhammad Ali

You may have to fight a battle more than once to win it.
—Margaret Thatcher

So the next time the Dow is down triple digits and you have a stack of client messages to return, or the production mountain seems impossible to climb, or when your mother is asking you why her account is down this month, remember: you too can be unstoppable!

32

'V' Is for V (FiVe)

At our firm, we have four production weeks most months, but about five times a year we have five (V to the ancient Romans). If this is how it works at your firm, what do you plan to do with that extra week? Instead of just making it a regular week, here are some ideas on how to make it special (and by the way, any of the five weeks can be the "extra" week).

If you do this right, and make it a "sharpen the saw" week, you can revitalize your business for the rest of the year. Here's the key: Just as a lumberjack doesn't worry about how many trees he's missing while he's sharpening his saw—he knows he'll chop down more trees in the long run—don't cry over your blade about the amount of business you might be missing during that time.

USE YOUR (EXTRA) TIME WISELY

- **Revive neglected accounts.** Do you have clients you've never met or seldom see? Plan a week of appointments to go see some of them, near and far. Meet them at an office in their area or at their homes. You may do some business right away, but if not, you'll create a more receptive client for the future.

- **Revive neglected muscles.** Get an hour a day of exercise. Even walking. And if you say you don't have time, remember that you just freed up at least 40 hours, which divided over those five weeks comes out to one hour and 36 minutes per day. Don't worry about how you'll do this next month. Just do it for this month, and then see how a good walk improves your stamina and energy.

- **Revive your business.** Monday, spend the entire day out of the office reading a book on practice management, time management, investments (Graham and Dodd maybe?), or selling. Tuesday, revise your business plan for the year. Wednesday, spend the entire day in a successful financial advisor's office, seeing what she does. Thursday, clean up and organize your office. Friday, go to a library and spend the day reading and planning what you will do to enhance your "belief" system.

- **Reinvigorate your client records.** Check out Chapter 15, "'E' is for Excel" for a way to create your own excellent database for anything you might want to sort and list.

- **Design and plan four client campaigns.** Take a manila folder, and tape a lined sheet of paper to the right hand side. List all of the people you would like to call on this product/service/idea. Then inside the folder, place all the relevant information about the campaign, from client positions to S&P reports. Then work one of those campaigns each of the four other weeks of the month.

Once you make use of this Vth week, you'll emerge from the year victorious!

33

'W' Is for Women

Although the ratio is changing, it's still the case that the majority of financial advisors are men. Yet since women often control the investments in a family—and are said to have most of the wealth—it might be worthwhile to have a little discussion about how women think and feel about financial matters. I'm speaking mostly to the guys here, since the only surprise for female advisors will be that men don't already know this stuff.

BRIDGING THE GENDER GAP

Gaining more understanding of how women communicate should help us relate to our female clients (and maybe even our wives) a little better. I claim no special understanding of the differences between men and women, except that I am one of the former and have read about and studied the communication style of the latter. Forgive the unavoidable generalizations, but see if some of it makes sense to you.

(Again, men reading this may think, "I didn't know that," while some women reading it will exclaim, "Well...duh!"):

- **Talking over problems: Tension versus relief.**

For men, talking about a problem is tension creating, whereas for women, talking about a problem is tension relieving. A male advisor's response to the problem of an account value being down might be to say, "Don't worry about it; it will come back up." Our inclination is to stay away from tough subjects and problems, or at best, to go think about it by ourselves. Psychologists call it "going to our cave." Talking about it just seems to make it worse to us.

Not so for our female clients. The very act of discussing their account, whether any solution is reached, relieves their tension. So, if our goal is to retain that client, we should make a call to talk about the investment problem. The good news is you don't have to have the solution before you call, because just the act of talking about the investment problem provides much of the solution in itself.

- **Whole picture versus compartmentalizing.** Women see the whole picture at once, whereas men put everything into little modules in our heads. Here's a book title that says it all: *Men Are Like Waffles, Women Are Like Spaghetti.* Men tend to have everything in separate mental compartments, like a waffle, whereas for women, every strand of spaghetti is touching every other strand all the time—it's all integrated. Another writer has explained that for women, it's as if 20 computer screens are all open at the same time, and they can see all of them. Whether it's from the way we're made, or some biological hunter-gatherer difference, our brains are wired differently.

My client, "Dorothy," with a $600,000 account, has been with me through thick and thin. Yet she still brings up a $2,000 investment mistake we had 15 years ago. It's not because she's trying to be difficult. Rather, it's because she sees everything about our investment relationship at the same time. That is just as real to her as the current state of the stock market.

One advisor went by a disabled client's house and helped her turn off a sprinkler that had gone haywire. Now, that didn't improve investment results. He was only trying to be helpful, not get more business. But in the client's mind, that added a new—very positive—scene to the overall picture of their investment relationship.

- **Conceptual versus linear.** Our female clients, because they see everything as a whole, may find it helpful when we cover an issue in different ways, rather than going through it in a straight, linear fashion. In talking with a male client about an investment, we sometimes progress through a mental checklist. Yield—check. Tax benefits—check. Safe—check.

With a woman, we might find it useful to cover whatever is most important to her from different angles. For example, rather than just mention safety once, handle it several ways. Talk about the AAA rating. Later in the conversation, mention how happy another client has been with the stability of the investment. Finish up with your philosophy about why it is important to find safe investments.

- **Insight: Financial plans incorporate most of what our women clients look for.** Why? Financial plans or holistic reviews involve talking about their financial problems and goals. They are, by nature, "whole picture" instead of compartmentalizing. The planning process lets clients talk about individual investments or insurance in the context of what they mean to their relationships. The entire financial planning process is conceptual instead of linear. Women prefer to see the concepts of financial planning, asset allocation, and future income needs all tied together in one place. And finally, the combination of graphs and spreadsheets makes all the concepts more easily understood for both genders!

Most guys are neophytes at understanding these concepts. I'm still learning, but my beautiful wife, Wanda, suggests that I may be making progress! (At least I think that's what she said—just kidding.) Besides the *Spaghetti/Waffle* book, other excellent choices to get some perspective on cross-gender communication are *Men Are From Mars, Women Are From Venus* and *You Just Don't Understand: Men and Women in Conversation.*

34

'X' Is for X-Roads

At some point in our careers, we all face a fork in the road: one path leads to burnout, the other to greater success. To be sure you choose the high road, consider these seven steps.

One definition of insanity: When you keep doing the same thing you've been doing, but hope for different results.

If you're not as excited about coming to work each day as you used to be, if you dread many of your client calls, if prospecting makes you think of panning for fool's gold instead of new clients, then maybe you're at a crossroads in your business. You may discover that it's time to re-examine your practices and see whether your daily activities match the pleasant dreams you had in those misty-eyed days of training.

Ask yourself:

- Would I rather eat a live toad than talk to several—or many—of my clients?

- Is each day like a Gordian knot that is never untied?

- Have my presentations to clients become as rote and unimaginative as a politician's stump speech?

- Am I keeping track of the number of contacts I make?

- Am I mentally burned out and unable even to imagine discovering one more new client's investment goals?

If you've answered "yes," you may be open to the idea of taking a higher and better road, where the air is cleaner, the grass smells better, and the view is fantastic, rather than continuing along this wagon trail eating other people's dust. The choice is yours; the turnoff to the high road opens up every day. Here are some ways that other advisors have found the high road:

1. **Read a book.** Three books that can absolutely revitalize your business and your life if you read them and follow their ideas are: *The Game of Numbers*, by Nick Murray, *Happiness is a Serious Problem*, by Dennis Prager, and *The 80/20 Principle*, by Richard Koch. For more ideas, see Chapter 12 "'B' Is for Books."

2. **Set up a system to increase your contacts.** The first four words of this phrase are the most important. "Increase your contacts" can be difficult. "Set up a system" is easy. Here's how: Give another advisor your car keys, not to be given back until you've made 25 (or 10 or 50) contacts that day. Here's another way: Hire a phone connector—someone to sit there and do nothing except call prospects and clients until they are reached, and who puts them through to you. That short-circuits the problem of call reluctance completely, and gets you out of the minimum wage work of dialing a number and waiting for the other party to answer. (And don't think you have to be a big hitter to do this. Thirty years ago, I received a call from a rookie who had someone call for him, say, "Hold for

Mr. Goldman," and then put him through. Maybe you can divide your time with another rookie and call for each other.)

3. **Plan your day.** Spend 15 minutes at the end and 30 minutes at the beginning of each day planning. This simple exercise will help you accomplish your priorities—not those of other people. Beware the sadness of working on other people's priorities.

4. **Hire a business coach.** Two to four times a month, spend time with a coach who will help you set goals—and hold you accountable for them. Even top-level athletes hire coaches. Why not you?

5. **Don't answer your own phone.** I learned from a multi-million dollar producer never to answer my own phone. This top producer returns every single call, but never lets anyone stay on hold. He stays in charge of each and every contact so that he can choose with whom he talks and how long. Beware the tyranny of the urgent!

6. **Hold small seminars.** If appropriate for your area, start holding small lunch seminars in your conference room. Invite enough clients and prospects so that you have eight to 10 people every Wednesday for around eight weeks. This will help you connect with them and pick up new referrals; it will also force you to brush up on your investment information and presentation skills.

7. **Give away accounts that make your life miserable.** (And this is the only time you will find me calling our clients "accounts.") Then take a deep breath. You will

be astounded at how much stress will vanish from your life. You'll wonder why you didn't do it years ago. The debate still rages over whether smaller accounts should be kept or given away, but each of us has accounts of all sizes that make our lives—and those of our support people—miserable. In fact, become a hero to your assistants by bringing them into your office when you make the call. Give these folks away, and hope that someone else can work with them better. There is not enough business anyone can do that justifies periodically ruining even a single hour of your day.

35

'Y' Is for You

Years ago, my teenage son York arrived home from a trip to Washington, D.C. wearing a T-shirt featuring the slogan, *"You don't know me."* Below the large-print words, an official-looking government seal read "Federal Witness Protection Program!"

How many of our clients come into our office wearing an invisible T-shirt saying "You don't know me" or "You don't understand me"? How many of our family members wear that same T-shirt? As Stephen Covey, author of *The 7 Habits of Highly Effective People*, suggests, "Seek first to understand, then to be understood."

As a financial advisor, you know that this entire business revolves around you and your clients. There's an old saying, "Nothing happens until somebody sells something; nothing happens until somebody buys something." However, you won't sell anything, even yourself, if you don't first understand your clients. And your clients will never buy if they don't feel understood. Understanding is the keystone of a successful, ongoing relationship with all of your clients, family, and friends.

GOODBYE TO "I"

One way to shift the focus from yourself to your clients is to get rid of the "I's" in your life. A friend of mine who runs a small manufacturing company forbids anyone in his company to begin a sentence with the word "I" in a business letter. He says getting rid of "I" completely changes the character of every letter, putting the spotlight on the recipient of the letter rather than the writer.

Somewhere I saw a list of the most important phrases in the English language:

- The most important word: You

- The least important word: I

- The two most important words: Thank you

- The three most important words: I was wrong

During economic crunch times, investment firms have proven they can do without certain departments. Some are scrapping their institutional bond traders, investment bankers, and even their training departments. But they can't do without the revenue producers. The top 5% of people in any field are never unemployed. They bring in the business because they focus on the "you" in relationships—to the exclusion of the "I." Their clients feel understood and valued, and they show their satisfaction by sticking with their trusted advisors through good markets and bad.

So the next time your client (or your child) wears that invisible sign that says, "You don't know me," consider it a red flag: they're clearly not feeling understood. Once you focus on them, they'll focus on you. After all, the people we value are those who value us, aren't they?

36

'Z' Is for Zone

Ever had a day where everything went right? Each client you called followed your suggestions? You asked three or four people for referrals—and actually received them? You could do no wrong?

On days like this, you're "in the zone." Pitchers talk about being in the zone when they are throwing a no-hitter. Tennis players talk about it when they win point after point and make seemingly impossible shots. Speakers talk about it when every comment elicits exactly the right audience response.

I'm sure you've experienced it. Can you imagine how successful you would be if you were in the zone every day? The people at the top of our profession weren't born that way. They're able to get into the zone for several hours a day—day after day after day. The rest of us—well, we might get into the zone for an hour or two once a month.

What's their secret? How do they get—and stay—in the zone for extended periods of time? From my experience, top producers follow these five steps:

1. **Congruence.** In his seminar "Insight on Time Management," Charles Hobbs says that, to be a success at managing your time, your lifestyle needs to reflect your core values. He recommends taking some time to determine what is important to you. Then, each morning, before you begin work, organize your activities to align them with these values. Someone asked him, "What do you do if you are operating out of congruence with your major values in life?" His answer: "Suffer." After all, as important as it is to get into the zone each day, it's even more important to be in the zone in your life.

2. **Consistency.** The next time you find yourself in the zone, suggests business coach Joe Lukacs, make some quick notes about what got you there. He calls these "Success Rituals." Did you arrive early? Create a list of people to call the night before? Exercise in the morning? Read a motivational book, or listen to a tape?

Review your goals and business plan? "You must determine what rituals or activities put you in a productive state," Lukacs advises. "A successful life is nothing more than the accumulation of a series of successful days."

3. **Confidence.** If those in the zone share any single characteristic, that characteristic is confidence. When you're in the zone, you could "go looking for Moby Dick in a rowboat and bring the tartar sauce along", according to Zig Ziglar! What gives you that confidence? Following your success rituals? If so, make a list and check them off. Wearing your favorite suit? Buy four more just like them. Do whatever it takes to find the confidence you need, no matter what the expense. Consider how much it costs you per day not to have that confidence.

4. **Concentrate.** No one knows better than you how many distractions rear their ugly heads during the course of your day. Have you ever played the Whack-A-Mole arcade game? The one where you put in a quarter and, as moles pop up, you whack them with a mallet? Ever feel like that in your office? That's OK if you get paid for killing moles, but if your job is recommending investments, it's a distraction.

To be in the zone, you need to concentrate. Make an effort to push off your distractions until after 4 p.m. every day—or, even better, to delegate or eliminate them. I know a top producer who drinks two or three cups of coffee a day; rather than sally over to the coffee machine and risk getting caught up in small talk, he keeps a thermos on his desk. He also makes notes on a pad of paper that his assistant picks up several times a day. She responds by writing notes back—that way, neither of them interrupts the other.

5. **Commit.** Once you determine what puts you in the zone and keeps you there, commit to doing those things every day. Stick to that commitment and you'll find yourself blowing that horsehide by the batters, making those impossible baseline shots, and moving your audience to laugh, cheer, and throw babies in the air. Most importantly, by sticking to your commitment, you can duplicate your best day as a financial advisor— every day.

This concludes our series of chapters based on the letters of the alphabet. Next, we begin a series of 3,000 chapters organized around the characters of the Chinese alphabet!

37

Thirty-Eight Reasons to Be Happy You're a Financial Advisor

Ever feel like the markets, the media, and your prospects are all conspiring to break your will? If so, you're not alone—we all get a little discouraged from time to time. If you have a case of the blues, consider this list of 38 reasons to be happy you're in the financial advisory business. You'll be re-energized before you finish reading.

1. There are great, motivated people all around you—take inspiration from them. Look around your office, around your community, even around the nation. Consider people in our industry and outside of it. I met a couple last Sunday who had raised 55 foster children! Just talking to people like that makes me feel motivated.

2. Remember when clients thought they could invest online and do better than you? The investments they made look horrible now. You shouldn't have a hard time getting those accounts back.

3. There are bound to be tax law changes that will cause people to seek your advice. Retirement plans have much higher contribution limits than just a few years ago.

4. Some investment made money last year.

5. Some investment will make money this year. Might be bonds, might be REITs, might be emerging markets, or something else.

6. In a down market, you have fewer competitors than you did one, two, or three years before.

7. People in our business do the right thing, by and large. If a prospect shows you her statements and you see that her other advisor has done a good job, tell her—you'll be rewarded for it.

8. Everyone you know knows 200 people, and some of them need your help.

9. As my operations manager says, "How about the great choice and diversity of investments available? Everyone should be able to find something they feel comfortable with. Unlike people who work only in real estate, insurance, or bank CD's, you can find ways for people to make money, even in equities, whether the market goes up, down, or sideways."

10. Plus, your quiver holds more than equities. You could have a successful career from this point on and never touch equities again. I wouldn't advise it, but that's one of the benefits of the range of products and choices we have.

11. You haven't met your best client yet!

12. You're going to see Dow 20,000, 50,000, and maybe even 100,000 one day.

13. New people are being added to the ranks of the wealthy every day.

14. You still have something to learn.

15. You can create goodwill by giving small gifts, such as pocket calendars or books you enjoy, to clients and centers of influence.

16. Mutual funds that you have forgotten about are paying you 25 basis points right now, and every night as you sleep!

17. There are stocks, including REITs, utilities, and others, that pay 7.2%. At 7.2%, your money doubles every 10 years.

18. You can use income investments that are relatively neutral if interest rates go up. Consider short-term government funds, step-up CDs, and TIPS.

19. We've experienced market volatility before. Talk to people who have been through this, ask what they did, and ask them whether it helped their business or hurt it in the long run.

20. There are things you can do now that you can't do when the market is hot—buy low, for instance.

21. You know more about investments than you did a year ago. I do—and I've been doing this since 1980.

22. You have incredible outside resources, from weekend seminars, to websites, to business coaches.

23. You have a reason to read inspirational books and listen to motivational tapes—activities that are among the most fun and potentially productive of those available to us.

24. Remember that kites rise against the wind, not with it.

25. Look at the obstacles you have already overcome.

26. Sir John Templeton once told me that the real standard of living has quadrupled in his lifetime, which has never before happened in human history. Kids now live better than kings of 200 years ago.

27. You've won life's lottery by living in the United States, Canada, or really anywhere in the developed world. Warren Buffett says that at the time of his birth, he only had a 1 in 50 chance of being born in this country. Society pays well for his skills. If he had been born a few hundred years ago, or in a different place, he says, he probably would have been eaten by a lion.

28. Your office is heated in the winter and air-conditioned in the summer.

29. At the time of this writing, a very wise investor friend of mine, Doug Peart, reminds us that mortgage payments are at a historic low. That means clients have more money available to invest.

30. You can earn fees on your client's loan business.

31. Inflation is amazingly low.

32. You could help a client earn hundreds of thousands of dollars over their lifetime with one piece of well-timed advice, such as "spend income, never principal" or "save 10% of every dollar you earn." Small efforts can produce great results.

33. Dividends are higher. This is partially a function of stock prices, but dividends on stocks are higher than a year ago and are benefiting from tax-friendly legislation.

34. Adversity has led to better tools. I don't know if you've noticed, but I think the print information from money managers, from investment companies, and probably even from your own firm has gotten better and better.

35. Annuities are better. Insurance companies have created enhanced "living" guarantees for clients. If you haven't considered them in a while, it may be time to take a fresh look.

36. You've already survived the hardest part. As the stock market continues to improve, you can be in a position to benefit.

37. You have better clients than you did a year ago. Most of those who were interested in short-term speculation rather than investing for the long term are gone. You have a core group of investors who value your expertise and are sticking with you.

38. You're better than you were a year ago. You know more, you're tougher, and you're more determined. You can't wait for next month. Bring it on!

38

Ten Ways to Defy the Doldrums

Having a little trouble getting motivated these days? If so, here are 10 real-world action steps you can take right now to jump-start your business:

1. **Watch another advisor for a day.** If you've never done this, you'll be amazed at how common your problems are—and how different your solutions. I'm still surprised that more advisors don't do this. Call ahead for permission before your visit. Don't ask questions. Don't interrupt. Just watch and take notes. You'll leave with a whole new outlook on your own business.

2. **Read a book on your business (not on investing).** Try Nick Murray's *Behavioral Investment Counseling*, or Maribeth Kuzmeski's *85 Million Dollar Tips for Financial Advisors*.

3. **Visit your client's place of business or civic organization.** This works much better than asking clients for referrals. Go where they are; meet their friends and co-workers. Find out how they make brass-plated wid-

gets. Sing a few songs at a Rotary Club breakfast. Or meet them for lunch at their neighborhood hangout.

4. **Compare your salary with earnings in other professions.** Here's a start: my college-age daughter worked 10 hours a week for 10 weeks last quarter and earned $700. You can earn that with one phone call. Alligator wrestlers in Florida: $12.50 per hour. (Nobody at the other end of that phone is as dangerous as an alligator.) Skip a shoot-around if you're NBA player Latrell Sprewell—deduct $125,000. Skip an office meeting—miss a sandwich. Deliver one million packages for UPS (about how many a driver delivers over 25 years); retire with a $60,000-a-year pension. Make one million dials to prospects or clients—priceless.

5. **Update and learn how to use better any software programs you work on regularly.** Some say that the worst day fishing is better than the best day working—and similarly, any tool you use is better than one you don't.

6. **Visit a retired client who lives at least an hour away.** Think of this as "Tuesdays with Morrie."

7. **Make an audio CD.** Put your best presentation about you and your firm on paper, get the required approval, and record it. Burn those CDs and integrate them into your marketing campaign.

8. **Go to a continuing education class with accountants or attorneys.** Find out what classes these professionals are attending for continuing-education credit, and attend one yourself. You'll meet some new

referral sources, find out more about what their concerns are, and maybe even learn something.

9. **Write a letter to your clients.** Concisely state your core investment beliefs. Write thank-you letters to people who have done business with you in the past two weeks. Tell clients what you are committed to doing for them.

10. **Form a mastermind group.** Get together with three to five other top advisors outside of business hours. Admission ticket: One business-building (non-product) idea. I promise you that you'll hear about stuff you didn't even know existed, from people facing the same problems you do, in your own language.

39

How to Run Your Day Like a Top Producer

It's mental focus that separates the top producers from the also-rans. It's true in any business, and it's especially true for advisors: top producers create excellent days by focusing on the daily activities they need to accomplish, whereas the less successful focus on a daily production number.

How far would a farmer get if he dug up the peanuts every day to see how they're growing? Does the professor give the final on the second day of class? Does the weight-lifter expect to be buff after just one afternoon at the gym? No. Greenjeans tills and hoes, the professor keeps giving her lectures, and every would-be Arnold is dedicated to his daily reps. They know that if they stay on task, results will come eventually.

Of course, advisors have so many disparate activities to handle that we sometimes feel hard-pressed to decide what to do next. Our job can be as difficult as herding cats. And not only do we have a huge mix of things to do, we also can find ourselves constantly distracted by that big goose-egg where our production number or new client number should be.

One time-management consultant commented that although he studies most professions for a week at a time, advisors do so many different things that he can only study us for two days at a time without driving himself batty. Imagine how we feel!

Yet the people in our field who live at the top of the mountain, where the air is fresh and the view fantastic, somehow seem to finish each day with satisfied contentment. They stand behind their desks, arms akimbo, and declare, "I am amused at the simplicity of this game. Bring me your finest meats and cheeses!"

So, you're thinking, how do we become one of these arms-akimbo guys at the peak of the mountain? By focusing on the activities, rather than the results. We know we can swing the bat 100 times, walk two miles this morning, or close our door and dial up 20 prospects.

IMPORTANT BUT NOT URGENT

My recommendation: Make a list of discrete actions that are important to your business. Include a lot of those tasks that Stephen Covey calls "Quadrant II" activities—tasks that you know are important but not urgent—they won't generate business today. Create a daily check-off sheet of these.

This could include doing something special for one of your top 20 clients, reading your business plan, reviewing client statements, or writing a note of appreciation to someone. Then—and this is really key—set a certain number of those activities to accomplish every day.

Don't try to do all of them in one day. You might list 20–30 items, and make a commitment to accomplish 10 of them.

Get 10 "points," if you will. Do that every day without fail. Advisors who try this find that it is fun, rewarding, and that it keeps them on track all day. As they focus on these tasks, they invariably find that they accomplish more, their production goes up, and their level of stress goes way down.

Below is a short list of the kind of activities I'm talking about. I use a Daily Stats list that I customize and change as my business changes:

- Prepare call list before day starts.
- Listen to motivational CD or audio.
- Exercise.
- Take some quiet time.
- Review business plan.
- Contact 12 clients/prospects.
- Contact another five clients/prospects.
- Ask for a referral.
- Throw away or handle eight inches of paperwork.
- Schedule a seminar.
- Add 10 quality prospects to prospect list.
- Set one appointment.
- Meet with one prospect/client.
- Plan with client service assistant.

WHAT YOU MEASURE, YOU IMPROVE

Transposing a record of your daily activities to a monthly statistics sheet lets you warehouse those numbers for a month-by-month comparison. In addition, the very fact that you know that these are going in your "permanent record" (remember how they warned you about that in school?) can motivate you to finish strong at the end of each day.

For self-actualizing people like us, it can actually be painful to write down what we consider to be low numbers. And recording digits that make you feel proud create a sense of accomplishment in a hard day's work, even if you're not seeing results yet.

Your firm may supply you with wonderful numbers, rankings, and charts. They can tell you how much fee-based business you have, how much business you do in each product, how many clients and households you have, and so on. This data can be helpful, but no one is going to keep track of the steps you've got to take to reach your goals, the daily actions that ultimately add up to success.

So, prepare an Excel table for yourself to record a month's worth of information, one day at a time. Not only will you wish to record your activities—such as contacts and referrals—and a rating for the day, but you will also want to add other numbers that are not tracked anywhere else.

I add columns such as "dollars brought in" and "trails hit" The first lets me track significant new money that clients have brought in, and the second lets me record managed money and mutual fund fees that hit. I can also track fees that aren't distinctly recorded anywhere else, such as trailers on annuity business or commissions for clients who make monthly mutual fund purchases directly with the fund. These are probably useful numbers for you, and if you have a goal to reach a certain amount of fee-based business, this gives you a way to track it.

Lastly, to bring it all together, have some totals rows at the bottom, as well as some averages, so that you can see how you performed for the month. Record these daily, look at your monthly totals and—following a simple idea from business coach Joe Lukacs—print these sheets and place them along with your daily stats sheets in a loose-leaf binder. You can refer to them at any time.

Sound too complicated to pull together? It's really not, and someone within earshot of you can help you do it.

Remember these two keys to the top-producer mentality: Focus on important tasks, not a daily revenue number. And record the incremental steps you take each day. You'll create a sense of accomplishment every day that will keep you energized as you progress toward your larger goals.

40

Battle Through the Day-to-Day Difficulties

There are a few memorable first lines in books. "Call me Ishmael," from *Moby Dick*. "It's not about you," from *The Purpose Driven Life*. *The Road Less Traveled* begins with the assertion that "Life is difficult." Dr. Peck then goes on to suggest that many of our neuroses stem from our habit of avoiding proper pain.

At any given moment, some advisors may be having record months, while for others, the current path isn't the one they chose in those misty-eyed days of training. Let's review some practical "how to's" of confronting and overcoming obstacles:

- **Make unpleasant tasks a habit.** Sure, we don't work in the coal mines or muck out stables, but sometimes a chore can seem that bad. The way to get through any unpleasant task is to make it a habit so you don't have to anguish over whether to do it or not. To quote from one of my favorite books, *The Greatest Salesman in the World*, "any act with practice becomes easy. Thus a new and good habit is born, for when an act becomes easy through constant repetition it becomes a pleasure to perform and if it is a pleasure to perform it is man's nature to perform it often. When I perform it often it becomes a habit and . . . since it is a good habit this is my will."

- **One bite at a time.** This is the answer to the old question, "How do you eat an elephant?" Or if eating elephants isn't motivating, how about: How do you build your castle? One brick at a time. Move a mountain? One stone at a time. Take a 3,000-mile trip? One step at a time. We certainly can take one step.

- **You are an "obstacle overcomer."** If people would invest as they should without any education, prompting, or even, yes, selling from us, then neither they nor the investment world would need us. The markets would move up to a point that people would receive a nice, stable return (3% maybe), and the people you stand in line with at the DMV could do your job.

  However, human nature doesn't work that way, and sometimes we need to convince folks to invest contrary to how they feel. We have to help them avoid the obstacles that the markets and life will throw in their path. That's why they call us advisors.

- **10 by 10.** I heard this a long time ago, and it still makes sense. Strive to contact 10 clients or prospects by 10 a.m. This 10-by-10 rule builds momentum and starts something good for the day. As they now say at the Indy 500, "Ladies and gentlemen, start your engines."

- **Put a price on each contact.** One financial advisor discovered that each contact with a client, prospect, or center of influence was worth about $200 in production to him. He found that as he increased his absolute number of contacts, that figure went down slightly but that it never averaged less than $100 per contact. How many phone calls would you make if someone were sitting across the desk from you giving you $100 bills each time you reached a client or prospect? Or even $20? $5?

- **Reward yourself for activities.** Dr. Aaron Hemsley, author and psychologist, suggests that one way to break out of a slump is to replace the dread in your mind with positive thoughts and rewards. He suggests putting a pile of paper clips in a cup and placing that next to an empty cup. Suppose that contacting 10 potentially unhappy clients is the task you keep avoiding, and you're feeling bad about it. If you even think about calling one of those clients, give yourself a reward by moving a paper clip to the empty cup. If you look up the phone number, give yourself another paper clip. If you think about how good you feel about those two paper clips, give yourself another paper clip. In no time at all, you'll be rewarding yourself so much and so fast, and feeling so good about it, that the actual calls will be a breeze.

- **Reframe your thinking.** When my son York was working on the climbing merit badge one day at Boy

Scout camp, he struggled more than he had for most of his achievements. But he kept going until daylight was gone, until his fingers were so raw that he had to wrap them in the only tape he had handy, black electrical tape. In his mind, he told me later, he knew that he would always remember the result of this day, and he wanted to be proud of what he overcame.

Like this, you can reframe your thinking to give you some extra motivation when times are tough. Have an unhappy client? "IBM built their reputation not by never needing repairs, but by being incredible at solving problems. This is a chance to prove how great my service is!" Are people hanging up on you? "Boy, I'll bet this is driving some of my competition out of the business!" Did the market drop 200 points today? "I can't believe what great prices we're getting on our dollar-cost averaging! We're sure going to miss these prices one day!"

Life is difficult. While that would bother a weaker person, it doesn't bother you—right?

41

Opportunities Abound—Even in Down Markets

I received the following e-mail from an advisor about an article I wrote outlining why this is a great time for us in our business:

Dear Bill,

There are times when it is not appropriate to be optimistic. Was it right to be optimistic two and a half years ago on stocks at much higher prices?

—Arthur A.

Here's my response:

Dear Arthur,

Thanks for reading and responding. It's always appropriate to be optimistic, it seems to me, but that's not the same as expecting the stock market to go up. A few years ago, when the market was zooming, I spent most of my days telling people not to expect the returns they were experiencing to continue, to move some money to bonds, and so forth. If one listened closely to Dr. Jeremy Siegel and Warren Buffett, they were saying the same thing.

It's appropriate to be optimistic about our lives, for all kinds of reasons—including the fact that, as Sir John Templeton says, the real standard of living has quadrupled in his lifetime, which has never happened before in such a short period of time in human history. By virtue of living in this country, at this time, and of being healthy and in an industry with un-limited potential—an industry in which, to a great degree, we determine our own future—we have already won life's lottery.

I recently reminded a client who has $3 million of house-hold assets that she is in the wealthiest one-tenth of 1% of all people who have ever lived. She's probably in the top 1% in this country. Surprised, she asked, "Why don't I feel that well off?" I replied, "Because everyone else you know, in this com-munity, is doing just as well as you are!" I further explained to her that the poor in our country live better than kings of 200 years ago, with better food, better health care, and more op-portunities.

Back to the stock market. Even at low levels, stocks sell for about 5-10 times what they were 20-30 years ago. If we don't like stocks, we can buy bonds, CDs, puts, or annuities; we can charge people for financial planning; or we can select any one of a zillion ways of doing our business. The opportunities are unlimited.

An advisor I know has done so well in his own account in the past six months that he recently paid cash for the home of his dreams. That's the purest example I've seen lately of someone creating wealth out of nothing but his own brains, experience, and guts. And his clients are prospering even more. He certainly doesn't think we've run out of opportunities.

Good question. Thanks for letting me respond. And thanks for reading!

—Bill

42

Sixteen Reasons to Be Happy When the Market Is Down

"You don't care, because you guys make money buying and selling whether the market goes up or down!" So burst out my retired client when I reacted with equanimity to a recent drop in the market. No point trying to explain it to him at that moment, because he was reacting emotionally, not logically. But that wasn't the reason that I was smiling.

I find it astonishing that some of my fellow advisors react with dismay when the market is down. I suppose it comes from a combination of fear about their own money, regret over promises or implied promises they've made to clients (and having to talk to those clients), and somewhere, the feeling that lower prices on investments must be unequivocally bad.

But the way I see it, an advisor being unhappy about a down market is like a farmer being unhappy because winter comes, or a surfer being unhappy when the tide goes out. It's irrational and useless to fight natural cycles.

SO BAD IT'S GOOD

It's easy to understand the happiness that comes when the markets are up. We can expect a number of nice experiences:

- Our existing clients are happy, thank us, and usually bring us more money.

- When we add up our net worth from our statements, we feel good.

- Few margin calls.

- More money to invest, and therefore higher fees.

- With a higher number, it appears that our clients will hit their goals sooner in terms of educating their children and retiring early.

All this may be true, but equally wonderful things can happen when the market—or stocks, or any other investment—is down. And I'm not talking just "eat your vegetables" kind of good things, but uniquely great things that you can only do when the market is down. Just as the farmer welcomes winter as a time to prepare his equipment, so the advisor should have a useful agenda for the fallow season.

I can hear your objections now, so let's take for granted that many more good things happen when the market is up than down. Let's say it's in a ratio of 4-1. So out of all the good things that happen to us as advisors, 80% happen when the market is up, and 20% happen when the market is down. Isn't that 20% worth exploring, especially since we are bound to be in a down market about 20% of the time? May I humbly suggest that you copy this chapter and place it under the calendar on your desk, as a ready reference when you're tempted to get negative in a "bad" market? Because here are 15 positive results and opportunities of a down market:

1. **Become a proven genius.** You told your clients it would happen sometime, right? So they get to see you as a genius who correctly predicted that sometime in the future their portfolio would be worth less than it was when they first invested, or at some temporary high point. You did, tell them that, didn't you?

2. **Play the role of able captain.** Clients look at you with awe as, like the captain of a ship on a stormy sea, you remain on deck, confident, and unworried, because you've been through many storms before. Your relationship with them is strengthened and you have the opportunity to talk and write letters to them explaining how you handle these storms. When the captain is back on shore, nobody wants to hear about the storms he encountered. They just have one question: "Did you bring in the ship?"

3. **Stand on the shoulders of the greats.** The greatest investors welcome these times. Shelby Cullom Davis, was one of two people to make it onto the "Forbes 400 Wealthiest Americans" purely on his own investment ability. (Warren Buffett was the other.) Davis said, "You make your money in bear markets. You just don't know it at the time."

4. **Separate the wheat from the chaff.** You get to look back at what various investment mavens said when the market was high, and see who was truly giving unbiased advice rather than shilling for investment firms. (Hint: Read Dr. Jeremy Siegel's *Stocks for the Long Run* and Warren Buffett's annual report letters.)

5. **Sign up satisfied clients.** The new clients you acquire at these times will be your most satisfied ever. Think of those you acquired in the spring of 2003, or 2009, and how happy they are.

6. **Eliminate competitors.** When the market is up, you get a lot of new competitors. When it is down, competitors leave the business and you can increase your market share in your community. In a down real estate market, how many fewer mortgage brokers and real estate agents are there in your city?

7. **Develop character.** Ok, one thought in the "eat your vegetables" category. Dealing with adversity makes you stronger. Oprah Winfrey was fired from her first job as a reporter. She was described as being "unfit for TV." Seems like she proved them wrong, didn't she?

8. **Take advantage of dollar-cost averaging.** As clients save and invest in their 401k plans or other savings vehicles, or receive stock options or deferred compensation, they get a wonderful opportunity to buy cheaply. And after all, when they retire or need the money, the market's going to be at "X", so every downdraft gives them and you an opportunity to buy more shares when the market is low, at some fraction of "X."

9. **Remember that obstacles = opportunity.** These obstacles and downdrafts actually create the value for your work. If markets only went up on a consistent, regular basis, you would be paid minimum wage for doing your job.

10. **Read St. Nick.** You get to read Nick Murray again, and remind yourself why you never, ever, give predictions or projections about the market or sell your services based on performance. "In the short to intermediate term it's unknowable; in the long term it's inevitable," he says. And "I don't know which direction the next 20% move in the market will be. But I am absolutely certain about the direction of the next 100% move in the market."

11. **Be aware of open ears.** Some investors who thought your advice superfluous become willing to listen to you after having caused considerable damage managing their portfolios on their own.

12. **Reap tax benefits.** You can take tax losses. Don't laugh. My very best investing client is ecstatic when

the market is down, because he knows he can stock-pile losses to use against the inevitable gains later. After about our first 18 years working together, having compiled a tremendous record of growth, and retiring at 55, he mentioned to me one day that he had never paid a capital gain on any of his stocks. True!

13. Investments are not Beanie Babies. Remember when Tyco Beanie Babies were bid up to hundreds of dollars? Remind your clients that stocks are not whimsical names, but shares of ownership in great American and international businesses. The Sage of Omaha, Warren Buffett says, "In the short term, the market is a voting machine, but in the long term it's a scale."

14. 100,000 to 1: Keep it in mind. You think that a few of your clients are unhappy? The ratio of the number of clients you have to the number of prospects in the world who need you is much less than 1 in 100,000. So at the worst, for every unhappy client you may have, there are 100,000 new prospects for you. In a down market, these prospects get antsy because they are unhappy with what they have been doing on their own or with another advisor.

15. Profit from panic. As for all the investors who don't have advisors as good as you (or whose advisors are on-line or on television)—let them panic. Your clients who are buying need someone to sell them shares, right?

43

Twenty-Two Things Your Clients Care More About Than the Market

Our clients talk with us about the market much as they would talk sports with a sportswriter over dinner or describe their bum knee to a doctor at a party. But we do them and ourselves a disservice to think that their happiness revolves around their investment performance. That's a bigger burden than we need to bear. It only takes a conversation with a client whose daughter just got into Juilliard, for example, or one who's just heard the word "cancer," to remind us that there are many, many more important priorities in their lives:

1. Their health.

2. Their family's health.

3. How their kids are doing in school.

4. Success in their job (or keeping their job!).

5. Misplacing their keys.

6. Losing weight (How many would gladly trade a 10% drop in the market for a 10-pound weight loss?).

7. Relationships with family members.

8. Fly-fishing, quilting, golf, lawnmower racing, or other hobbies.

9. A big tax bill (the market may come back, but those tax dollars never do).

10. Bragging about the tomatoes in their garden.

11. Their religious or community organization (Ever heard that old story about the business executive who lost "everything" in the crash of 1929? Looking out his window in despair, he saw a group of children walking to an event at his church, and was comforted when he realized that the only money he hadn't lost was what he had given away.)

12. Property values increasing.

13. Company coming over for dinner tonight.

14. A bad night's sleep.

15. Their next vacation.

16. Home repairs.

17. Whether their estate is set up correctly.

18. Their favorite NFL team's quarterback controversy.

19. The current Dick Francis/Mary Higgins Clark/Tom Clancy novel they're reading.

20. Auto insurance premiums going up now that their son is 16.

21. Personal safety.

22. The future of their country.

So maybe we can lighten up a little, not carry such a large burden, and have clear-headed, rational discussions with clients about their investments. It's not life and death. It's only money.

44

How Much Are You Really Worth to Clients?

Ever hear the story about the six-year-old who kept tossing a baseball in the air and attempting to hit it? Every time he threw the ball, he'd yell, "I'm the greatest hitter in the world!"—and then he'd swing the bat and miss. Finally, he paused a minute, and with the wisdom of youth, threw the ball into the air and yelled, "I'm the greatest pitcher in the world!"

Recently, I ran across a prime example of how this kind of redefining of terms sheds a wonderful light on what we do. What's more, I discovered mathematical, statistical, unequivocal proof that what you and I do for a living is the single most important determinant of our clients' investment success. Think I'm overstating it? Here's what I found:

In its materials on the discussion of performance measurement, the Investment Management Consultants Association (IMCA) discusses the difference between dollar-weighted returns and time-weighted returns. Apparently, in the early 1970s, the Bank Administration Institute issued several precepts, one of which is still accepted today: "The impact of the size and timing of capital flows must be eliminated in assessing manager performance since these flows are not within the manager's purview."

In other words, the time-weighted rate of return should be used rather than the dollar-weighted rate of return. IMCA elaborates more on its rationale a few pages later: "Time-weighted rate of return eliminates the effect of client-initiated additions and withdrawals that are beyond the control of the manager. The result is an accurate and unbiased measure of investment performance that is the same with or without cash flows."

As the Church Lady from "Saturday Night Live" might say, "How convenient!" Well, maybe that works fine in defining money managers' performance, but it specifically excludes the most important determinant of a client's success: our advice. The act of persuading clients to be in the market— successfully encouraging them to stay even when they want to flee—is the absolute biggest factor that determines their investment performance.

QUANTIFYING OUR VALUE

Let's talk numbers. Investor advocate John Bogle says in a July 8, 2003, *Wall Street Journal* article: "The returns incurred by the average equity fund investor since 1984 have averaged just 2.7% per year, a shocking shortfall to the 9.3% return earned by the average fund. The result is that the average fund investor has earned less than one-quarter of the stock market's 12.2% annual return." Ever year, this number is updated, but the ratio remains about the same.

As you and I can confirm, these figures are attributable to fact that the average investor failed to get into the market until near the top, pulled out after it had gone down, over-emphasized the wrong sectors based on recent performance, and so forth. So a professional financial advisor—who did nothing more than keep his client's money in the market in good mutual funds or managed accounts during that time—accounted for 6.6% a year of the client's performance. That means that a $100,000 investment would have grown to $541,730 instead of $165,897, for a difference of $375,833. (By the way, it's worth noting that in his article, Bogle, as is his tradition, focuses on the 2.9% difference between 12.2% and 9.3%, rather than the much larger 6.6%.)

Your clients may have made over a third of a million dollars because you made those calls, convinced them to invest in the market when they could have stayed in high-yielding CDs, and persuaded them to hang tough during the bear markets that occur about every 3-5 years. My friends, that dwarfs any difference in manager performance over that time. It's a more important number than alpha, beta, the Sharpe ratio, the Sortino calculation of downside variance, the Stochastic calculus, and the Treynor ratio. It's more important than the expense ratio of a fund (with apologies to John Bogle) or the amount that's charged in 12b-1 fees. In fact, it's more important than all those other calculations put together, for two reasons:

1. It's a bigger number.

2. It reflects the real world and the real experience of investors.

STAKING THE CLAIM

Therefore, I hereby name this figure the "Smith ratio" and define it as the difference between Dalbar's report of the average stock fund investor's dollar-weighted, real-life return and what your client experienced because of your help (her dollar-weighted return). So for that 19-year period, the Smith ratio for an investor whose advisor kept her fully invested would be 6.6% a year, for a total of $375,833.

Doesn't this warm the cockles of your heart? What you do on a daily basis—by knowing your clients, by executing proper financial planning principles, by persuading them to stick with what is right rather than running with the sheep (or the lemmings!) —is the most important determinant of their investment success. You've always known this, but let's put a name to it and talk about it. That's why they need you, and that's the purpose you fulfill every day. I feel honored to be working alongside all the unsung investment professionals who are the real factor in determining investors' wealth.

45

Six Plagues That Advisors Conquer—Always!

Pine beetles saved my house from the California wildfires.

As I sit here in my front room on a Sunday morning, out of my window I see burned shrubbery peeking through the fog. A burned-up utility trailer is in the foreground. It sits next to a pile of ash and engine parts that fell from my daughter's exploded SUV before it was towed—or more accurately, dragged off.

What I don't see are the remains of eight 40-year-old pine trees. I don't see them because we cut them down last summer. And therein lies the story.

We loved the beauty of those pine trees. We enjoyed summers under their canopy. My wife and children picnicked under them when our kids were small. One evergreen held in its branches a nest of golden eagles. How blessed we felt to be able to watch as they raised their young and taught them to fly, two fledglings the first spring, and three the next.

A TOUGH DECISION

But last summer, after 20 years in our home, we cut these evergreens down because they were infested with the western pine beetle. The pests first hit the majestic pine that hosted the eagles' nest. Then they struck the adjacent tree, then the next. They finished by killing two pine trees that were directly in front of our home, which dropped their needles in big piles in front of our windows.

Although we regretted having to cut down these trees, we went ahead and paid thousands of dollars to have them completely removed. There was nothing we could do to save them. We stopped just short of cursing the pine beetles.

You may remember seeing the California wildfires on television October of 2008. More than 500 homes were destroyed within a few miles of us. After seeing the speed at which the flames were moving, we left our home at 2:30 in the morning. As the 50mph winds pushed the fires through the valley below us, they blazed through a neighboring canyon, destroyed two homes, then flashed across our grove as they sped toward the next canyon.

Our row of 28 cypress trees went up with the sound and speed of firecrackers, according to our neighbors who stayed. The fires burned every tree, shrub, and vehicle in their path. Apparently, flames came right up to our front door and stopped, because even the doormat was singed.

But thank God, except for some smoke damage, the house remained untouched, as you can see above.

Now to the pine beetles. If the pines had not been infested by these insects, we would have left them standing. If we had not cut down the trees, they would unquestionably have lit up like blowtorches and fallen on our home, crashing through the roof. Although we drove off in two cars filled with pictures and family memorabilia, we would still have lost many irreplaceable mementos and family heirlooms.

Is it OK to thank God for a bug? I hope so, because we do. The insects, which we initially saw as pests, saved our home. What appeared to be a problem, a difficulty for us, turned out to be a blessing.

WHAT'S BUGGING YOU?

Our family is not the first to be thankful for insects. In the center of town in Enterprise, Ala., stands a statue to the boll weevil. The boll weevil is and was a terrible pest that in the pre-pesticide era destroyed cotton crops. Cotton was the cash crop for most farmers in the area of Enterprise, and this bug decimated their livelihood.

So why build a statue to this pest? Because the destruction of their cotton crop caused these Alabama farmers to look for another crop, and now farmers in south Alabama make a good living from growing peanuts, among other hardy plants. The farmers commissioned the statue because they realized they never would have gone that direction had it not been for the boll weevil.

Have you ever thought about the boll weevils and pine beetles in our business? How about these:

- **Rejection.** None of us like to have people reject us. But if our careers involved no rejection and clients came to us in a steady stream, frankly, there would be no need for what we do. Certainly we would not be compensated at the high levels possible in our profession. Our jobs could be handled by clerks paid about as much as someone behind the counter in a retail store.

- **Bad markets.** These seasonal pests actually give people a chance to make money. If the markets went up at a steady pace, they would be bid up to the point that the returns went down to CD rates. Picture a kid playing with a yo-yo while riding an escalator up. In times of market volatility, everyone is focusing on the yo-yo, while advisors help people focus on the escalator.

- **Responsibility.** How many bright, caring, good looking people have you known in our industry who know as much as you do about investments but would pale at the thought of taking responsibility for someone else's money? Do you realize how unusual you are in that you can handle your emotions and advise people effectively even when their anxieties are pushing them to do the wrong thing?

- **Paperwork.** Advisors may feel it's always in danger of overwhelming us, but paperwork actually keeps us in business. Now you and I would always do the right thing for clients, but without compliance paperwork and good record keeping, some of our compadres might be tempted to take shortcuts. In that case, we might never have met some of our best clients. Without these pesky industry rules and paperwork, clients may have been cut off at the pass and led astray by someone who was exaggerating or misleading.

- **Unpleasant clients.** First, these "canaries in the coal mine" sometimes alert you to service shortfalls that nicer, more polite clients keep to themselves. You should thank them just for that, if nothing else. Second, they give you a chance to grow in character as you remain calm and unruffled despite their maelstroms. Third, if they become abusive with your staff, you get to play the hero when you protect your staff by talking to or even firing the clients.

- **Income uncertainty.** This bug alone keeps 90% of your would-be competitors out of our industry. As you find ways to do business and take care of your clients through any adversity, your character and courage become stronger. Learning that you can overcome this monthly uncertainty through your own resourcefulness causes your confidence and faith in yourself to grow. And in my case, every month of pulling success from uncertainty also increases my confidence in the One who sends these pine beetles to help us along.

46

How Top Achievers Overcome Failure and Rejection

I heard the voice message and immediately recognized the distinctive voice, even though I had never talked with the speaker in person. "Bill, this is Art Mortell. Thanks for mentioning me in your article... Call me if you get a chance."

He wouldn't have had to tell me who he was. After years of listening to his recordings in the early morning while I was running or driving to work, his voice is one of a few, including my own father's, that I can hear giving me advice in my head when I face a tough decision.

Mortell's recordings and his books *The Courage to Fail* and *World Class Selling* share a lifetime of experience, both his own from his career at IBM, and from stories he has gathered. He speaks with humor, conviction, and enthusiasm. Since he has spoken to people in our industry for decades, many of his stories are about financial advisors.

In his motivational stories, he describes valiant souls who have overcome seemingly insurmountable personal or business failures. A child who was disabled by polio, yet became an Olympic champion. A mountain climber who fell down a crevasse and was left to die, but crawled his way back to camp. A businessman who lost his business and all his money at the same time his wife left him, but survived and rebuilt his life. He describes what these people thought, what they told themselves, and how they came back to great success.

If there were a Nobel Prize for Intelligent Motivation, Mortell would have received a medal in Stockholm years ago. What he writes is scientific, real—not just sappy positive thinking. May I suggest, brother and sister advisors, that this is an opportune time for us to go back and review some of his articles or lectures about overcoming rejection and failure? You can start with his free articles at www. artmortell.com. I like "Becoming More Resilient" as well as "There Are No Bad Days."

WHY THE TIME IS RIGHT

As this is written, most advisors could use a shot in the arm. Remember: it's not just you; every advisor out there is facing what's probably the toughest market of their careers. Here's why we need Mortell's wisdom now more than ever:

1. **We have experienced failure as client portfolios have tanked.** We may continue to experience failure and rejection as we lose accounts. We know people who will have to wait longer to retire now, or who will have to adjust their standard of living, whether they're our own clients or people in our social circles. And no one is really talking with you about how to deal with that in your own head. Even a strong market recovery, by itself, will not patch up your psyche.

2. **The worst may be yet to come.** Bear markets can feel bad, but many an advisor has a worse production drop the next year. Understand: that production drop occurred after the market began to recover. Up until that point, many had enjoyed double-digit increases in revenues every year. It took a while after the market recovered, however, for investors to be so ready to get back into the game. To deal with and overcome that, good mental preparation could be helpful.

3. **Rising markets make many advisors fat and happy and allergic to facing rejection.** Before the downturns, we weren't rookies anymore and could talk only with people who liked us and would seldom take issue with our recommendations. We were in a comfort zone. We could go a week or a month without anyone saying no or disagreeing with us. Wasn't that nice?

   But we're never going to grow out of tough predicaments by staying comfy. It's time for us to get back out there, face people who are going to say no, and talk to people who need our help. It's time to make it into a game again and rescue people from their own mistakes.

MAKING GOOD USE OF FAILURE

Personally, I find it a strange paradox that at the time in my career when I know the most, look the wisest (gray hair and glasses), and am least likely to face rejection, I am most unwilling to do so. Since we may have hundreds of millions dollars under management, how could one little rejection possibly hurt us? And no matter how many clients we have, there are a hundred times or a thousand times that many investors in our own communities who are unhappy and looking for answers right now:

- Read Art's book *Enjoy Failure, Be Amused by Rejection, Thrive on Anxiety...and benefit from whatever happens,* with the following quotes giving you a flavor of what to expect:

- "Whether we experience failure or success is unimportant; what is important is the way we deal with the experience."

- "Most of us will succeed only to the extent we are willing to suffer through many disappointments."

- "We begin to succeed when we learn how to fail."

- "Trauma becomes humorous when converted into a war story."

- "Failure is only an experience that is less than we expected."

- "Decide how failure, rejection, and anxiety enhance your self-image."

Thanks, Art!

47

Four Ways Top Producers Show Clients They Care

A while back, my friend Phil Smith died after a long bout with cancer. He was a fine man, a former NBA All-Star, a community leader, a father of five, and even an investment advisor at a national firm for a few years. I'd see him fairly regularly—at church, for example, or when our kids played soccer against each other. Our daughters, both named Amber Smith, laughed about being frequently mistaken for each other.

Soon after Phil died, I ran into two of his former colleagues, both 20-year veteran advisors. Our conversations gave me some important insights into what constitutes a successful advisor—and what doesn't. Here's what happened:

The market-focused advisor

I bumped into the first advisor at a community event.

Advisor #1: "Hi, how are you doing?"

Me: "Well, thanks. Did you hear that Phil Smith died? I think his memorial service is this Friday."

Advisor #1: "Yeah. Where do you think the market's going? I think the S&P is going down to 350. You know, I'm more of an economist than a broker. I converted to fee-based business, but I'm only getting about 10 basis points and..."

The people-focused advisor

I saw the second advisor the following day, while taking a stroll through a local park.

Advisor #2: "Hi, Bill. Would you do me a favor and make this market go up tomorrow morning?"

Me: "Sorry, I can't. Not through buying yet. Hey, did you hear that Phil Smith died?"

Advisor #2: "I saw that in the paper. What a tragedy! He was a great guy. They're having a service for his family later this week, aren't they?"

Me: "Yeah, I think it's Friday at 1 p.m."

Advisor #2: "Such a shame for his family. We used to play basketball in some civic leagues together. As you can imagine, he was very good. I remember when he was prospecting NBA players...."

SHOWING CLIENTS YOU CARE

One of these two advisors is near the top at his firm; the other, while a good guy, left the business. Can you guess which is which? And can you guess why?

Advisor #1 seems to lack interest in people—and if that's so immediately obvious to me, it's probably clear to his clients as well. Advisor #2, on the other hand, is tuned in to people—a trait that goes a long way toward explaining his status and success.

This might seem like an extreme example, but the lesson is clear: the best-performing advisors are not, ironically, entirely wrapped up in performance—what they care about is people. What's more, they take steps to maintain regular contact with clients, as well as to reach out on particular occasions or in times of need.

What about you? You might genuinely care about your clients, but are you sure that you've made your attitude apparent to them? Becoming caught up in daily nitty-gritty is easy—particularly in troubled markets. If you suspect that you're among the lax, consider the following four tips:

- **Learn all you can about your clients.** In *How to Swim With the Sharks Without Being Eaten Alive*, Harvey Mackay says that the salespeople for his printing company are required to complete a 61-item list of questions about their clients. Some of the information is basic—their kids' names, where they went to college, and so forth. Other details need to be sussed out over time—a client's hobbies, for example, and whether he prefers golf to fishing. Think how well this kind of information could serve us if we kept it in our contact files and used it to show interest in our clients' lives: "Didn't you go to USC? How are they going to do against UCLA this week?" Or "Is your daughter Whitney still in marketing?"

- **Invest in some small talk.** Preparing a financial plan or working on a financial checklist with people gives us a great opportunity—seldom experienced in our hurried world—to ask people about what's important to them. Watch—they'll stand amazed when you raise topics other than the stock or investment vehicle du jour.

- **Get a feel for their values.** Pose Bill Bachrach's question: "What's important about money to you?" Keep working on clients until they reveal their deep-seated feelings about what all this "stuff" really means to them. Always keep your focus in mind: not the numbers on the statement, but what those numbers can do to enhance the lives of clients you care about.

- **Show appreciation.** Remember: these clients are paying for our mortgages, our vacations, and even our children's education. Send personal thank-you letters after meetings, after clients bring in money, or for no reason at all. And if possible, thank them in person. I say something like, "I just want you to know that one of my great pleasures as a financial advisor is getting to know people like you."

Relating to our clients can be a lot more fun when we start looking at them as people, rather than as accounts. And it makes for a quantum leap in their loyalty, too.

48

Ten Talking Points for Rattled Clients

During a bad market, I asked a well-respected business coach what was on the mind of the advisors he coached. He responded without hesitation, "What do I tell my clients now?" Whenever markets go down, advisors at every firm throughout the country—whatever their specialty—struggle to come up with an answer to help their clients cope with seeing their statements priced so low.

We could try telling them that we cryogenically preserve their portfolios, and will unfreeze them when a cure for bear markets is discovered. Or that their statements were accidentally priced in euros this month. But if those two responses don't work, here are 10 real-world ideas from financial advisors who have sailed through several of these storms with their clients intact:

1. **Talk big picture.** One experienced advisor says: "The first thing I try to do is to get the discussion away from the outlook or target for any one company, or even the whole portfolio. Talking about what a good company

Microsoft is, or Cisco's next quarterly earnings, is part of what got us into this mess. I move the conversation away from their own portfolio to the larger market. Then they can usually think more clearly and less emotionally. Third-person stories from other people are the best, such as 'When Iraq invaded Kuwait in September of 1990, the stock market dropped quite a bit right away. One client told me that she was going to remain invested, even though she was a little worried. She was rewarded by seeing the market go up about 30% in two weeks in January of 1991, and was very glad that she stayed in.'"

2. **Reinforce their commitment.** From a 15-year veteran: "I like to remind them what legendary investor Bernard Baruch said: 'These are the times when shares return to their rightful owners.' You have to help people feel good that they are making a proactive, smart decision by staying invested in the market, and not just hearing excuses from you!"

3. **Deflate their rationalizations.** Another senior advisor tells clients about a hobby he has—he keeps a list of the things investors say at the tops and bottoms of markets. And it's always the same. "At the top, they say, 'This time it's different,' 'We're in a new paradigm,' or 'I don't see anything that could go wrong.' At the bottom, they never say, 'I'm going to sell out because I'm scared to death, I can't sleep at night, and this feels like a flesh-eating bacterium.' Instead, they sell everything and rationalize their decision with something that sounds better: 'I'm just going to get out for a little

while, because it will be next year before the market goes back up.' But that's a dangerous decision, because it never seems right to get back in."

4. **Avoid groupthink.** In July 1982, with the Dow at 800, an advisor who gives seminars fielded a call from a local economics professor. The professor asked him to speak to his class, but only about buying puts, because, "As everyone knows, the only way to make money in the market is to bet on it going down." He reminds his clients that the conventional wisdom is often—perhaps usually—wrong.

5. **Focus on the opportunities.** Another advisor counteracts clients' negative feelings with the opposite emotion. "These are great times!" "We're going to miss these prices in a couple of years." He tells clients that these are the very best of times. When they need the money, say at retirement, the market will be at X, no matter what it does in the meantime. The more chances they get to buy shares while they're on sale, the better off they'll be in the long term.

6. **Encourage independent thinking.** We all get the question, "What is the consensus about what the market is going to do?" One advisor's answer is that she doesn't know and doesn't care what people on television and in the newspaper are saying. "Were those people you see on television telling you that the market was going to drop when the Dow was much higher? So why listen to them now? They don't know what's going to happen, especially those who speak the loudest and act the most sure about what they are saying."

7. **Concentrate on the long term.** A veteran financial advisor says he tells clients what he has had to learn, from the father of value investing, Ben Graham: "Individuals who cannot master their emotions are ill-suited to profit from the investment process."

8. **Use visual aids.** One advisor says, "I have on my wall a picture of a little boy, circa 1965, with a very sad expression on his face as he contemplates his dinner plate with nothing left on it but broccoli and lima beans. The caption reads, "This is what buying low feels like."

9. **Get Warren Buffett to help you.** Still another advisor tells her clients Warren Buffett's story about his imaginary business partner, Mr. Market. It goes something like this: Imagine that you have a partner in business named Mr. Market. Mr. Market has some wonderful qualities. He always has money to buy your shares, and he is always willing to sell his shares to you at some price. Unfortunately, Mr. Market is not emotionally balanced. Some days he comes in bouncing off the walls, offering to buy your shares at an extremely high price, while other days he comes in weeping, ready to sell you his shares at a very low price. The one thing to remember is that Mr. Market is very emotional, and not to make the mistake of getting irrationally exuberant or utterly depressed along with him. Sell him shares when he offers you much for them, and buy shares from him when he is selling his shares cheaply.

10. **Draw parallels.** An advisor from Southern California offers this: "I talk with them about real-estate prices.

They all know that the price of their homes have gone up and down, yet they never considered selling them. I remind them that in our area, in 1989, you couldn't find anyone who had ever lost money in real estate. Then we went through an eight-year real estate recession, and by 1997, it seemed you couldn't find anyone who had ever made money in real estate! Then the pendulum swings back again. I let them make the analogy to the stock market."

Finally, remind clients that forbearance is a virtue. As one wise advisor once said, "Smooth seas never a great sailor made."

49

An Open Letter to a New Branch Manager

Dear BOM:

Welcome to our branch. We haven't met you yet, and we don't even know your name, but we look forward to some great times working together. You're taking on a job that many of us wouldn't want to tackle. Or, even if we wanted to, we probably couldn't handle it. You can count on our support and respect for you and your position. Our firm has already shown its confidence in you by making you a critical part of its growth and governance.

We look to you for many things, but here are some specific insights as to what will make the office run more effectively:

- **Be fair.** Rules you set up should apply to everyone, and you might as well realize that any special arrangements you make will come to daylight at some point.

- **Don't equate our value with our production numbers.** The 20- and 30-year survivors you see out there are the evolutionary 5-10% who have outlasted all the others, because of their ability to deal with clients, pick investments, and prospect. There are all kinds of ways of looking at this, but here are three. 1) Is the best surgeon for you necessarily the one who schedules the most operations? 2) Who benefits the firm more: the million dollar producer who costs a lot to bring over and who will change firms every four years, or the $500,000 producer who has no "deal" being written off? 3) Of all the financial advisors you've known, to whom would you send your Aunt Matilda with her life savings?

- **Don't spend all your time oiling the squeaky wheels.** Some of them will never be happy no matter what you do, while those who quietly and politely ask for help the first time will surely turn into squeaky wheels, if you force them to act that way.

- **There is no "I" in branch manager.** I've heard managers talking to other managers, saying things like "I was up 30% this year," or "I had a great August." Unless you entered every ticket in the branch, I would humbly suggest using the pronoun "we." Do this even if only other managers will hear you, because it does something to your own attitude to think that way. At least until the day I hear a symphony conductor say, "Did you hear how well I played tonight?"

- **People watch what you do.** Grizzled veterans might not appear to need your attention, but they will appreciate it. Make a tour of the office first thing each morning and check in with each person, if for no other reason than to let them know you're behind them.

It can be something as simple as, "How is your mother? You still have that cold? What big opportunity can I help you with?" Be aware of the appearance of the office and the actions of advisors. We're asking people with big money to come see us, and they expect an organized, business-like environment. Handle the things we can't, such as problems with a product area or some other issue where we need your influence to weigh in.

- **Realize how important you are in someone's life.** You will be nearly god-like—a father figure—to somebody. I've seen support people to whom a word of appreciation or a sign of respect (or the opposite) will be in their thoughts for weeks. For financial advisors in training, think of your own experience. How much influence did your first manager have on your life? How much did you learn from him or her? Have you ever heard Stephen Anderson, a legendary producer and industry trainer, talk about his first manager, the man who hired him when no one else would give him a chance? Have you ever heard Zig Ziglar talk about his life and how his career turned around when his regional manager said, "Zig, you can be one of the great ones?"

- **Think about the legacy you will leave.** I know a group of extremely successful insurance agents who were hired and trained by one Bill Malone, a sales manager who has probably been long since forgotten by everyone else at his company. Bill died decades ago. I never met him, but his widow is my client. I had heard about him from friends who were agents years ago. They would tell stories about what he taught them and the kind of character he had.

Here's proof of his influence: 20 years after his death, these agents still check up on his elderly widow to make sure she is doing well and to offer to help her any way they can. How would you like to be held in such respect that decades after you are gone, people are still offering to help your spouse or children because of what you did for them?

- **Get a life.** I have yet to go to a retirement party for an advisor or manager, but I've seen others leave this business in all kinds of unpleasant ways. Take care of your family, your health, and your mind, and encourage us to do the same. We'll all be around a lot longer, and enjoy it a lot more.

Sincerely,

Bill Smith

50

Eleven Ways to Eliminate Anxiety and Enjoy Your Job Every Day

Norman Vincent Peale, celebrated author of *The Power of Positive Thinking*, used to tell a fascinating story about a businessman who completely eliminated anxiety from his life. Dr. Peale said this fellow had been "the most anxious man in New York City. And that's saying something!" They saw each other weekly at the civic club to which they both belonged.

One day Dr. Peale noticed that the man was no longer nervous and tense. His anxiety seemed to have completely disappeared overnight! When Dr. Peale asked him about it, the man smiled and suggested, "Well, come to my office at the end of one day, and we'll go to dinner." So on the appointed day, Dr. Peale showed up at the man's firm and was ushered into his office.

The man greeted Dr. Peale, then asked him to wait a moment. He cleared off his desk, put a few items in order, then walked to the door. On the wall next to the door, he had a page-a-day calendar, and below that a wastebasket. He crumpled that day's page in his hand, closed his eyes briefly, and dropped the page into the trash. He turned to Dr. Peale and said, "Let's go to dinner."

At dinner, Dr. Peale asked him about whether this little ritual had anything to do with his relaxed and calm state. "Absolutely," the man replied. For years he had suffered from anxiety at work, never seeming to get everything done, and always worried about things he failed to get to.

So he began this end-of-day ritual of clearing his desk, then walking to the calendar. As he crumpled the page in his hand, he closed his eyes and said a short prayer that went something like this: "Lord, I did my best today. Whether I got it all done or left some things undone, today is over. Thank you for the day that has ended, and now I leave it all in your hands." Then he dropped the page for that day in the wastebasket, and for him, the day was over.

Sound silly? Maybe so, but in our industry, the top producers find a way to have a definite beginning and ending to the day. They work as hard as they can and do their best for that one day, and then put it to bed, knowing that tomorrow will offer them a fresh start. They know that if they don't, they will walk out the door anxious, tense, and perhaps not fully present for their spouse, children, or friends.

END THE NEVER ENDING WORK DAY

Early in my career, I had a business partner who had been a hard-as-nails Air Force pilot, then a commercial pilot for a major airline. The most difficult part of the job for Andy was not prospecting or making investment recommendations, but the fact that each day never seemed to definitively end. Long after he left the office, and well into the night, he would think about things he could have done or things he could do the next day. It bothered him, and it bothered his wife.

Finally, Andy went back to the airlines. He liked being a pilot because it demanded his full concentration from the time he walked onto the plane to do the preflight checklist until the time he walked off after the flight. But once he walked down the ramp into the airport, he was done. There was nothing else he had to think about until the next time he walked onto an aircraft.

No one rings a bell to tell financial advisors when their day is done. We don't punch a clock, turn an engine off, or even clean up a kitchen. And that lack of finality can lead to anxiety. If this is a concern for you, try some of these tools used by top producers to rein in anxiety and put parameters on their work lives.

1. **Focus on activities, not results.** In our business, we simply can't control the fees or commissions that we are paid on any given day. In fact, it's even worse than that. Sometimes we can do very little and be paid a great deal. Other times we work very hard and are paid nothing that day. An economist would say that in the short term, effort and results are poorly correlated statistics. So don't focus on dollars revenue that day; instead control what you can control.

2. **Track those activities.** Decide what the important activities are for you, whether it's asking for referrals, making client contacts, scheduling client meetings,

or whatever. Track your numbers daily, put them on a spreadsheet to add them up monthly, and check your trends. In the long term they do matter.

3. **Nuke the things that irritate you.** Tell me what your daily pet peeves are, and I'll tell you how to get rid of them. Any problem you have, someone not too far from you has figured out an answer to:

- Phone ringing constantly? Don't answer your phone. Return calls later, after your assistant or your voice mail has taken a message for you. First, most callers can be better handled by your assistant. Second, for the few calls that remain, you'll be better prepared. Third, do you want clients to class you with their doctors or lawyers—who don't answer their own phones—or with their auto service person who does?

- Wholesalers, other advisors, and clients walking in without an appointment? Tape a sign on your door that says, "Please do not interrupt. Working on client project until 12:00."

- Toxic clients? You already know what to do with them, right?

4. **Begin the day early.** Whether we are talking about wake-up time or office-entrance time, move it up. Whatever early means for you, get there. Almost nothing creates more anxiety at the beginning of the day than showing up after things have started happening and feeling that you're already behind.

5. **Set a closing time.** Without a firm closing time, you will procrastinate what you need to do all day. Decide when the office closes, and stick to your schedule.

6. **Have a closing ritual.** Thirty minutes before the end of the day, begin to make the next day's call list, clear off your desk, and pack up. Make sure the office looks as clean as you want your mind to be the next day.

7. **Help someone.** Almost invariably, our anxieties occur when we are focused on ourselves. Focus on someone else for a few minutes every day. Help a rookie in your office. Send a note of appreciation to your child's teacher or principal. Or better yet, send a note or make a phone call to one of your old teachers, coaches, or mentors. Remember the old adage "When a man is all wrapped up in himself, he makes a pretty small package."

8. **Be grateful.** Every person reading this is among the wealthiest 5% of people who have ever lived, and probably among the wealthiest 1%. Whether you consider yourself blessed by God or just a winner of life's random lottery, be grateful! Today in the United States and the West in general, we have quality food, access to modern medicine, convenient transportation, and tremendous opportunity. Appreciate it—don't get caught up in office nattering about this commission cut or that management decision. My philosophy, drawn from my own life, is, "It sure beats picking peas and beans under the hot Alabama sun."

9. **Reboot your thinking.** Read Dale Carnegie's *How to Stop Worrying and Start Living*, or Dennis Prager's

Happiness Is a Serious Problem. You will never think about your worries the same way again.

10. **Listen to something positive on your way to work.** There is plenty in the world that can cause you to worry. Inoculate yourself against that by feeding the good, the powerful, and the positive into your mind early in the day. Get some good CDs by Zig Ziglar, Earl Nightingale, or Art Mortell. You wouldn't start your day by eating moldy bread and rancid meat, would you? Take as much care in feeding your mind as you do in feeding your body.

11. **Live in a manner consistent with your values.** This is a longer-term ideal, but you have an opportunity every single day to be sure that your life and your actions support what you consider to be your most basic values. Anxiety invariably lessens when you are accomplishing what matters most to you in all areas of your life.

Implement a few of these tips to set up boundaries and routines that keep your work life manageable as well as successful. And as you're addressing the tough stuff, remember this calming advice from Calvin Coolidge, who said, "When you see ten troubles rolling down the road, if you don't do anything, nine of them will roll into a ditch before they get to you."

51

Turn Time Into a Tool—Not an Excuse

Recently, I participated in a conference call with renowned business coach and Horsesmouth contributor Joe Lukacs, from International Performance Group. The topic of the call was how financial advisors can consistently create an "excellent day." Joe started the call with three questions all of us should answer:

1. What would I do if I had 20% more time?

2. What price will I pay if I don't keep hitting excellent days?

3. Do I know the outcomes I desire?

One participant stated that he would ask for and follow up on referrals better. Another participant mentioned that she would spend more time with her kids.

After listening to the answers, Joe stated that, in his years of coaching financial professionals, he was completely unable to correlate time spent in the office and money earned. Finding more time—even, say, as much as 20% more time— isn't necessarily the answer. What we really need to do is increase our effectiveness in the time we do have. Here were his suggestions:

- **Use "flexible time-blocking."** Many advisors try to time-block. We plan, say, to spend from eight in the morning until noon calling clients. But as soon as something upsets the apple cart, such as a client who calls about his account, our system crashes because we have built no cushion or margin into our day. So we get frustrated and blow the whole system off. Build in 15- to 60-minute periods during the day in which you return calls or work on other projects.

- **Ritualize your mornings.** Move your start time up in order to have some cushion during the day. Top producers employ a success ritual at the beginning of every day; make sure you do too.

- **Cut down your to-do list.** People set themselves up for failure when they have a giant to-do list. They know they won't get to all of it, and the very action of looking at the list frustrates them. Instead, create three lists that will help you achieve small, quick victories throughout your day:

  1. A "must-call list," made up of people you will definitely call today.

  2. A "must-do list," consisting of no more than five to six items that will absolutely, positively be done today, leaving plenty of margin to do other things. (Not a "to-do" or "should-do" list!) FranklinCovey would call these your "A" tasks, and would say that you must limit that list to "life-sustaining" items.

3. A "project list" that includes all the other things you may work on at some time in the future. You may look at this list up to three times a day and even move an item or two to your must-do list, but you shouldn't keep it in front of you nagging your brain all day.

- **Establish an end-of-the-day ritual.** Just as you begin your day with a regular success ritual, finish your day with a consistent ritual. If you have 30 minutes or an hour before you leave, don't begin a new project for a client. Rather, clear your desk, make your call list for the next day, and put everything in place to achieve success tomorrow. Begin and end each day in an organized, consistent fashion. In other words, ease in and ease out.

The upshot of the conference call was that establishing consistent rituals can help you become more effective without working any more hours. Best of all, your "excellent days" will become much more frequent as your business grows and you achieve your goals.

52

Thirty-Nine Ways to Stay Upbeat

The market may be volatile, but you don't have to be. When circumstances have you tracking a downward slope, try one of these suggestions to get you back above your 50-day moving average, or even setting new highs:

1. Talk to positive people.

2. Don't let anyone dump garbage in your head. You wouldn't let someone walk into your home and dump a can of garbage in your living room. Why let them do that to your mind?

3. Remember that low prices are great for buyers.

4. Fine-tune your skills.

5. Consider that you have more choices of how to do your business than just about anybody else in any other industry.

6. Remember that you have a nearly unlimited choice of investments.

7. Turn off CNBC. They don't know, and don't know that they don't know.

8. Invite an upbeat speaker to your office.

9. Prospect.

10. Laugh.

11. Perform a random act of kindness—pay the toll for the next car behind you.

12. Call that friend who always lifts your spirits.

13. Listen to Zig Ziglar recordings.

14. Listen to Brian Tracy CDs.

15. Listen to upbeat music.

16. Challenge anyone who dares use the phrases "tough times like these," "in this kind of market," "times are slow," etc. I love the old Federated Funds commercial, where one guy says "I don't even look at my statements anymore, things are so bad." His lunch partner looks at him, puzzled, and asks, "What are you talking about?"

17. Challenge any client who says the market is bad—bad to sell or bad to buy?

18. Million dollar executives in tech companies get laid off; you don't.

19. Remember that when the going gets tough, the tough get going (not that these times are tough—see #17).

20. Think about how your clients' expectations are lowered and how happy they'll be with a 10% growth year now!

21. Read *Unstoppable*. If all you read is the story about Legson Kayira, who left his tribe in Africa, walked 3,000 miles, talked his way into a scholarship at a college in America, and later became a professor at Cambridge, it will be worth it.

22. Visit shut-ins or children in the hospital to get over your bad self.

23. Realize that at some point, this will be over, and you'll miss these prices, the time, the chances to prospect that person who is now unhappy with their financial advisor but won't be a year from now.

24. Think about all the online and discount trading firms that advertised against you and are out of business.

25. Repeat the title of Joe Namath's book to yourself, *I Can't Wait Until Tomorrow . . . Cause I Get Better-Looking Every Day.*

26. Remember that 50% of all doctors finished in the bottom half of their class.

27. Write yourself some affirmations. "Saturday Night Live's" Stuart Smalley says, "I'm good enough, I'm smart enough, and doggone it, people like me!" Al Franken is mocking the idea when his character says it, but he did become a U.S. Senator!

28. Remember the story of the hotdog vendor whose son went off to college, came back and told his dad that there was a recession on? Sure enough, his less-educated dad stopped advertising, worked fewer hours, and in no time at all business was bad!

29. Refuse to participate in any "theoretical" bad markets.

30. Remember that man is most comical when he takes himself too seriously (from Og Mandino's *The Greatest Salesman in the World*).

31. Ponder the words of inspirational poems "If" or "Invictus."

32. Tell your clients what I told mine after a trip to Africa: "If it gets really bad, we can live for $1 a day in Ethiopia!"

33. Make a list of all the incredible things you have accomplished in the past that would make other people say "Wow!" and review it periodically.

34. Get enough rest. As Vince Lombardi said, "Fatigue makes cowards of us all."

35. Brian Tracy says to silently repeat to yourself: "I like myself, I like myself . . ."

36. Get some exercise. That sends endorphins to your brain which give a feeling of well-being. Exercise > Endorphins > Euphoria.

37. Help someone else. Remember the old story about Hell being a place where everyone was starving in spite of sitting at a beautiful table set with great food. Each of them had two-foot spoons attached to their arms and couldn't get the food to their mouths. Heaven looked exactly the same, except that they were all having a great time and were enjoying the food because each person was feeding the person across the table!

38. Consider that it is this very volatility that can allow investors to achieve double-digit returns in the stock market. If cash returns 3% over time, and stocks return 10%–12%, then why would anyone ever choose cash? Because to get those higher returns, one has to be willing to suffer through terrible news, no guarantees, and the feeling in your gut that makes you need to drink from the pink liquid sometimes.

39. Remember the story about the twin 7-year old boys? One was invariably pessimistic and the other always optimistic. Scientists put the pessimist in a room full of great toys and he was still unhappy. They put the optimist in a room with nothing but a large pile of manure. After an hour they came back, and found him digging furiously into the pile. When they asked why, he replied, "With all of this manure, there's got to be a pony in here somewhere!" Find the pony.

53

Thirty Tips
That Propel
High Achievers

It is not the critic who counts: not the man who points out how the strong man stumbles or where the doer of deeds could have done better. The credit belongs to the man who is actually in the arena, whose face is marred by dust and sweat and blood, who strives valiantly, who errs and comes up short again and again, because there is no effort without error or shortcoming, but who knows the great enthusiasms, the great devotions, who spends himself for a worthy cause; who, at the best, knows, in the end, the triumph of high achievement, and who, at the worst, if he fails, at least he fails while daring greatly, so that his place shall never be with those cold and timid souls who knew neither victory nor defeat.

—Theodore Roosevelt

This quote from Teddy Roosevelt has been a favorite of high achievers for nearly a century.

It's packed with wisdom, but what would you say is the most important phrase in the quote? Most readers would agree that it is "The credit belongs to the man who is actually in the arena. . ." How about the second most important? I would suggest that it is "who errs and comes short again and again because there is no effort without error or shortcomings…" Yet when you see it in print, that phrase is often left out.

EMBRACING FAILURE

It seems to me that our generation is in denial about something that Teddy Roosevelt knew very well: High achievers err and fall short, fail, and crash and burn again and again!

In our profession, and indeed in all professions, high achievers don't insulate themselves from failure. Rather they welcome it and rack up many failures in the course of a day or a week. They know that they are able to accomplish so much precisely because they are willing to work through challenges such as prospects who say no, marketing campaigns that don't work, and thorny problems that hike their anxiety.

That's not to suggest that it's easy to power through failures. As one industry veteran put it, many of us, like weary boxers, tire of taking so many body blows. So how do we get ourselves to attempt things, without regard to whether we succeed or fail? In other words, how do we separate activity from results? Here are 30 effective strategies used by top producers; try them out for yourself and see how your stamina improves:

1. Remember something my friend Jim Christman said when I suggested I couldn't handle a particular mechanical task: "How do you know that you can't?"

2. Compile a list of things that you had never done before but succeeded at doing once you tried.

3. When you show courage, even in something small, record the date and the action.

4. When you tackle and succeed at something that seemed overly complicated to begin with, make a record of it.

5. Keep the previous three lists in a tabbed notebook and read that notebook daily in order to remind yourself of your capabilities.

6. Write up affirmations for yourself and read them out loud three times daily until your subconscious has absorbed them and they have replaced the "can'ts" that undermine you.

7. Practice being ridiculous. Eric Saperston graduated from college and camped around the country in a VW van interviewing famous people about their lives. Many people thought he was crazy, but in the end, he not only interviewed 300 successful people (actor Henry Winkler and the chairman of Coca-Cola, to name but two), but now runs a film production company with millions of dollars in contracts. Eric says, "When people think you're nuts, it gives you a wide range of behavior to take advantage of."

8. Develop and use an end-of-day ritual. That way, you will be able to close the book on each day, with all of its successes and failures, and you won't carry it with you.

9. Develop deeper relationships with your spouse, kids, and friends, so that you're cushioned against even

massive failure. Have many fulfilling aspects to your life so that business is not everything.

10. Determine how much each of your actions or dials is worth to you in dollars and cents (regardless of the outcome), and keep that figure written on a card in front of you. One advisor determined that her average outgoing dial, whether successful or not, was worth $50 in new business to her. Who wouldn't punch in a few numbers for $50?

11. Stop imagining other people are so together. They aren't! And we all should have stopped comparing ourselves with other people a long time ago, about the time we graduated from high school.

12. Create excellent habits, because then the daily decisions no longer have to be made. (Read or reread "The Common Denominator of Success," a 70-year-old speech that speaks as directly to us now as if it had been written yesterday).

13. Read or reread *The Greatest Salesman in the World*, by Og Mandino. Many advisors credit it with much of their success. So does the actor Matthew McConaughey!

14. When you face something that seems so complicated that you just can't get a handle on it, set a kitchen timer for 45 minutes and work on it for only that amount of time, then stop. You can do anything for 45 minutes. And you'll be surprised at how many of these monsters take only about 10 minutes once you get started.

15. Get a friend or two to work on the project with you. The Bible says that although one string can be broken, even a strong man can't break a rope with three strands.

16. Encourage someone else. Take the focus off yourself.

17. Memorize motivational poems such as "Don't Quit" (by an anonymous author).

18. Be audacious!

19. Do 10 things in the time others would procrastinate over one.

20. Put it all in perspective. What's the big deal?

21. Read or reread the great Nick Murray's description of putting quarters into a slot machine, knowing that they will pay off one day. It's in *The Excellent Investment Advisor*.

22. Be willing to take the time to solve any problem. Given enough time, an ant can carry away an elephant.

23. Develop consistent processes and write them down so that the anxiety of "how to do it" is no longer there after the first time.

24. Listen or relisten to Aaron Hemsley recordings such as "The Psychology of Maximum Sales Performance."

25. If you have to eat a live toad, don't sit staring at it too long! Call those difficult clients or handle those difficult problems early in the day. Own up to your mistakes early.

26. Adjust to changes, such as needing glasses or learning new software. Life changes. You change. Get over it!

27. Turn it all into a game. Keep score of the activities you do, which, along with your attitude, is really all you can control.

28. Collect a list of your favorite inspirational sayings, such as "The journey of a thousand miles begins with the first step" and "He who is outside his door is half-way there."

29. Read biographies of people who have weathered many failures on their way to success. Thomas Edison, Abraham Lincoln, Marie Curie, even Teddy Roosevelt. He didn't make that speech just because he was a witty writer. He said those things because he had lived them!

30. Have fun!

54

Lessons From the Christmas Cactus

Across the room from me, right now, is a plant known as the Christmas Cactus. It doesn't bloom all year, then suddenly blooms just before the end of December. My parents used to own a plant nursery, and I spent my teenage years moving way too many of these pots around. (There also exists a Thanksgiving Cactus, which blooms just before Thanksgiving every year, and an Easter Cactus....you get the idea. But back to the Christmas Cactus.)

If you saw this plant during most of the year, it would look like an ordinary and not very attractive plant. You might tend to use it for background, if you had a garden.

But something within the DNA of the plant tells it to sprout beautiful pink blooms at this particular time of the year. It relies neither on outside circumstances, nor on the skill of the people who take care of it. It is simply programmed to bloom. And no matter how unsuccessful it looks before blooming, it is going to bloom when its time comes, and nothing short of death will stop it.

WHAT ABOUT YOU?

If a plant, with no mental faculties, is programmed to bloom, then can we have any doubt that inside our own DNA is the program to bloom, to succeed, to contribute to the world? Maybe you've had great success in your career and your life so far. Is there still more that you're programmed for? Maybe you feel that you haven't achieved all that you want. Maybe so far, you've seemed ordinary, even to yourself, like the Christmas Cactus during the first 11 1/2 months of the year.

Yet isn't it possible that right now, this moment, this year, this month, is your time to be what you can be? Forget for the moment past frustrations, past failures, past discouragements. For most of the year, this cactus I see looks pretty drab compared with just about any other plants. Yet when I look around at this time of year, I see that all other plants have stopped blooming and the Christmas Cactus has come into its own.

WIRED TO BLOSSOM

You are programmed to succeed and to achieve everything you ever hoped for in this business, with your family, and in your life. As a financial advisor, you find yourself in a career with no limits except those you set yourself.

You're living in the freest country ever created, at a time of unparalleled human technology and wealth. Even the Declaration of Independence, the founding document of our country, tells us that we are "endowed by our Creator with certain unalienable rights, that among these are life, liberty, and the pursuit of happiness." In spite of great national struggles, you've seen our nation come through strong and determined again and again.

YOUR BLOOMSDAY

Your life will keep getting better and better. In "The Strangest Secret," the first spoken recording ever to sell a million copies, Earl Nightingale has said that "Life is rigged; not to prevent the strong from succeeding, but to prevent the weak from failing."

The Christmas Cactus is going to bloom at the right time, because its DNA is programmed that way. So is yours.

See you blooming.

55

New Year's Resolutions: Getting to $1 Million in the New Year

At the start of a new year, it's natural to set fresh goals and plan for a better year ahead. Here's what one producer is working on:

I will spend my time exclusively on $500-per-hour activities. A million-dollar producer is worth $500 in fees per hour to his firm, and much more than that to his clients. I will delegate and hire out $10-an-hour tasks. I can have it all, but I can't do it all.

I will read books or listen to audio recordings each morning in order to begin every day highly motivated.

I will read my goals and business plan at least once each day in order to stay focused.

I will determine who my ideal clients are, as well as which of my current clients fit that mold, who can be converted to that mold, and how many new "right" clients I need.

I will ask for a referral twice daily.

I will remind myself daily: Life is difficult. As M. Scott Peck wrote, in *The Road Less Traveled*, "All neuroses stem from the attempt to avoid legitimate pain." Or, in Nietzsche's words, "What doesn't kill me makes me stronger."

Every day, I will offer encouragement to another person: my wife, my kids, a client, another advisor, my kids' teachers, a center of influence, the guy at the gas station—someone.

I will strive to make each day an excellent one. Like Bill Murray in "Groundhog Day," I may have to live the day over and over in order to get it right, but once I do, I will labor to duplicate that accomplishment every day.

I will spend time weekly with centers of influence for the purpose of reminding them what I do and how I can help their clients. I will stay "top of mind." It's no coincidence that the products I remember are the ones whose wholesalers show up periodically in our offices.

I will ignore changes my beloved firm makes in pay structure and client account charges, since I have no control over that. Instead, I will see these changes as opportunities for my firm— and therefore for me—to become more profitable.

I will not depend on the market to rescue me, because to do so is to remain a victim.

I will have fun. I will remember the words of Dave Dean, sales trainer and motivational expert: "I'm not important, but what I become and the people I help are extremely important."

56

Wall Street Does Dylan's 'Don't Think Twice'

Sometimes a song playing in your head can really keep you going. Here's a Bob Dylan tune you might recognize—with a little word "Smith"ing—that might help keep you going through the end of any lingering bear. (The "Davis" mentioned is Chris Davis, and of course, "Buffett" is Warren Buffett.)

Don't Think Twice, It's All Right
(with apologies to Bob Dylan)

It ain't no use to sit and wonder why, guy,

It don't matter anyhow

And it ain't no use to sit and wonder why, guy

If you don't know by now

When the gavel hits at the break of dawn

Look at your screen and that bear'll be gone,

You're the reason he's traveling on,

Don't think twice, it's all right.

It ain't no use in sittin' there in cash, gal,

Cash is trash, don't you know?

And it ain't no use in sitting there in cash, gal,

While these bargains you forgo,

Still I wish there was something I could do or state,

To try and make you asset al-lo-cate,

You're gonna miss it if you hes-i-tate,

Don't think twice, it's all right.

It ain't no use in calling out those names, man,

Of all your stocks that are down,

It ain't no use in calling out those names, man,

'Cause you still can't make me frown,

I'm a-thinkin' and a-wond'rin 'bout Graham and Dodd,

And Buffett and Davis as they smile and nod,

They buy when it's cheap and not when it's mod,

Don't think twice, it's all right.

You're walking down that long, lonesome road, pal,

Where you're bound, I can't tell,

But good buys are there to be had, pal,

So I'll just say, "Buy and sell."

You might say stocks treated you unkind,

But now your prospect's scared to trade online,

There'll be a bull if you just give it time,

Don't think twice, it's all right.

Recommended Reading

Anderson, Lester, W. and Shelley, Lee, A. *You Are the Product: Powerful Self-Marketing for Practicing Professionals*, Financial Marketing Group, 1996.

Aurelius, Marcus. *Meditations*, Penguin Group, 2006.

Bettger, Frank. *How I Raised Myself From Failure to Success in Selling*, Fireside, 1992.

Bogle, John, C. "The Emperor's New Mutual Funds," *The Wall Street Journal*, July 8, 2003.

Bradbury, Ray. *Fahrenheit 451*, Simon & Schuster, 2003.

Bunyan, John [Author]. Pooley, Roger [Editor]. *The Pilgrim's Progress*, Penguin Classics, 2009.

Carnegie, Dale. *How to Stop Worrying and Start Living: Time Tested Methods For Conquering Worry*, Pocket Books 2004.

Collins, Jim. *Good to Great: Why Some Companies Make the Leap... and Others Don't*, HarperCollins, 2001.

Covey, Stephen, R. *The 7 Habits of Highly Effective People: Powerful Lessons in Personal Change*, Free Press, 2004.

David, Robert, C. *The Undaunted Life: How to Succeed No Matter What*, Bob David Live, Inc., 2010.

Farrel, Bill & Pam. *Men Are Like Waffles, Women Are Like Spaghetti: Understanding and Delighting in Your Differences*, Harvest House Publishers, 2007.

Ferguson, Howard, E. *The Edge: The Guide to Fulfilling Dreams, Maximizing Success and Enjoying a Lifetime of Achievement*, Getting the Edge Co., 1990.

Franken, Al. *I'm Good Enough, I'm Smart Enough, and Doggone It, People Like Me!: Daily Affirmations By Stuart Smalley*, Dell, 1992.

FranklinCovey: Leadership Training, Consulting and Management. http://www.franklincovey.com

Gerber, Michael. *The E-Myth Revisited: Why Most Small Businesses Don't Work and What to Do About It*, HarperCollins, 1995.

Gray, Albert E.N. "The Common Denominator of Success." Speech given at The National Association of Life Underwriters, 1940.

Gray, John. *Men Are From Mars, Women Are From Venus: The Classic Guide to Understanding the Opposite Sex*, Quill, 2004.

Hemsley, Aaron. "The Psychology of Maximum Sales Performance," Aaron Hemsley & Associates, 1998-2009. http://www.aaronhemsley.com

Henley, William Ernest. "Invictus." *The Columbia Anthology of British Poetry*. Woodring, Carl and Shapiro, James [Editors]. Columbia University Press, 1995.

Hill, Napoleon. *Think and Grow Rich*, CreateSpace, 2010.

Hobbs, Charles, R. *Time Power: The Revolutionary Time Management System That Can Change Your Professional and Personal Life*, HarperCollins, 1988

Kersey, Cynthia. *Unstoppable: 45 Powerful Stories of Perseverance and Triumph from People Just Like You*, Sourcebooks, Inc., 1998.

Kipling, Rudyard. "If." *The Collected Poems of Rudyard Kipling*, Wordsworth Editions Limited, 1994.

Koch, Richard. *The 80/20 Principle: The Secret to Success by Achieving More with Less*, Double Day, 2008.

Korn, Donald and Gross, LeRoy. *The New Art of Selling Intangibles*, Marketplace Books, 2003.

Kuzmeski, Maribeth. *85 Million Dollar Tips for Financial Advisors*, Red Zone Publishing, 2004.

Mackay, Harvey. *Swim with the Sharks Without Being Eaten Alive: Outsell, Outmanage, Outmotivate, and Outnegotiate Your Competition*, Ballantine Books, 1996.

Mandino, Og. *The Greatest Salesman in the World*, Frederick Fell Trade, 2001.

Mortell, Art. "Becoming More Resilient." http://artmortell.com

Mortell, Art. *The Courage to Fail: Art Mortell's Secrets for Business Success*, McGraw-Hill, 1992.

Mortell, Art. *Enjoy Failure, be Amused by Rejection, Thrive on Anxiety... and benefit from whatever happens*, Dynamics of Human Potential, 2010.

Mortell, Art. "There Are No Bad Days." http://www.artmortell.com

Mortell, Art. *World Class Selling: How to Turn Adversity into Success*, Dearborn Trade Publishing, 1991.

Murray, Nick. *Behavioral Investment Counseling*, The Nick Murray Company, Inc., 2008.

Murray, Nick. *The Excellent Investment Advisor*, The Nick Murray Company, Inc., 1996.

Namath, Joe Willie and Schaap, Richard. *I Can't Wait Until Tomorrow...'Cause I Get Better Looking Every Day*, Random House, 1969.

Nightingale, Earl. "The Strangest Secret." Nightingale-Conant, Inc., 2008. http://www.nightingale.com

Peale, Norman Vincent, Dr. *The Power of Positive Thinking*, Fireside, 2003.

Peck, M. Scott, Dr. *Further Along the Road Less Traveled: The Unending Journey Towards Spiritual Growth*, Touchstone, 1998.

Peck, M. Scott, Dr. *The Road Less Traveled: A New Psychology of Love, Traditional Values and Spiritual Growth*, Simon & Schuster, 2002.

Prager, Dennis. *Happiness Is a Serious Problem: A Human Nature Repair Manual*, Regan Books, 1998.

Roosevelt, Theodore. "The Man in the Arena." Speech at the Sorbonne, Paris, France, April 23, 1910. http://www.theodore-roosevelt.com/trsorbonnespeech.html

Sarno, John, Dr. *Healing Back Pain: The Mind-Body Connection*, Warner Books, 1991.

Schwartz, David, J. *The Magic of Thinking Big*, Fireside, 2007.

Shelley, Percy Bysshe. "Ozymandias." *The Columbia Handbook of British Poetry*. Woodring, Carl and Shapiro, James [Editors]. Columbia University Press, 1995.

Siegel, Jeremy. *Stocks for the Long Run: The Definitive Guide to Financial Market Returns & Long Term Investment Strategies*, McGraw-Hill, 2008.

Stanley, Thomas, J. *The Millionaire Next Door: The Surprising Secrets of America's Wealthy*, Pocket Books, 1998.

Tannen, Deborah. *You Just Don't Understand: Women and Men in Conversation*, Harper Paperbacks, 2001.

Warren, Rick. *The Purpose Driven Life: What on Earth Am I Here For?*, Zondervan, 2002.

Ziglar, Zig. *See You at the Top*, Pelican Publishing, 2000.

ABOUT THE AUTHOR

Bill Smith is a financial advisor and widely read columnist at Horsesmouth. His Uncommon WYSdom column is known for its blend of practical and motivational insights into what it takes to succeed with clients and prospects, while maintaining strong ties and support from family and community. He is involved with the Alzheimer's Association, the Salvation Army, Rotary International, and Free Wheelchair Mission. Bill is a graduate of Auburn University. He and his wife Wanda are the parents of three grown children and live outside of San Diego.

INDEX